PALETTE
mini
GOLD & SILVER

First published and distributed by
viction:workshop ltd.

viction:ary™

viction:workshop ltd.
Unit C, 7/F, Seabright Plaza, 9-23 Shell Street,
North Point, Hong Kong
Url: www.victionary.com
Email: we@victionary.com
🅕 @victionworkshop
🅨 @victionary_
🅞 @victionworkshop

Edited and produced by viction:ary

Creative direction by Victor Cheung
Book design by viction:workshop ltd.
Typeset in NB International Pro from Neubau

ISBN 978-988-79034-1-3
Printed and bound in China

3

PREFACE

According to the Cambridge Dictionary, the word 'palette' may refer to the range of colours that an artist usually paints with on a canvas. Today, however, more than just the primary means of creative expression for wielders of the physical brush, its role has expanded to include that of an important digital tool for crafting meaningful solutions in design. On top of manifesting pure works of the imagination as it has always done, the palette has become a purveyor of infinite visual possibilities with the power to bridge art and commerce. Since the release of its first edition in 2012, viction:ary's PALETTE colour-themed series has become one of the most successful and sought-after graphic design reference collections for students and working professionals around the world; showcasing a thoughtful curation of compelling ideas and concepts revolving around the palette featured. In keeping with the needs and wants of the savvy modern reader, the all-new PALETTE mini Series has been reconfigured and rejuvenated with fresh content, for all intents and purposes, to serve as the intriguing, instrumental, and timeless source of inspiration that its predecessor was, in a more convenient size.

INTRO

As commerce slowly became the biggest cog of civilisation, the role of gold and silver grew more prominent in society as tokens of wealth and vanity. Due to the increasing levels of difficulty with which they can be found and mined from the natural environment today, the two precious metals have remained symbols of opulence and sleek sophistication respectively; particularly when they take the form of jewellery, luxury items, and decorative objects. However, with increased accessibility to advanced technology over time, modern designers have devised creative ways to manipulate even the smallest bits of the materials to add lustre to their pieces, whether through plating and coating techniques to make surfaces shine or gilding and engraving for textural enhancements.

Unlike colours perceivable under normal circumstances, gold and silver visibly come to life when they gleam and shine. Designers typically have to be sensitive when applying them onto visual outputs so as to achieve the right balance between distinction and distraction. For 'The Kaleidoscopic Eye' by Mori Art Musem and Thyssen-Bornemisza Art Contemporary, ujidesign studio were inspired by the nature of the exhibition itself to stimulate the senses through the interaction of light. Their collateral design on page 142 showcases a generous use of silver with dotted text to demonstrate the exhibition's concept and reward audiences with subtle glints when the materials are moved. Catherine Renee Dimalla's cover design work for the 48th edition of Jeopardy magazine on page 434 also plays with light through clever lattice-work and pattern placements reminiscent of ancient Mayan motifs. Gold was chosen to reference the latter's culture, mark the year of the publication itself, and celebrate the talents featured within.

Due to the easy way with which gold and silver can channel their inherent associations and characteristics, a designer can go all out to grab the target audience's attention. In Foundry's VIP invitation design project for luxury retailer Liberty's Fashion Renaissance event on page 292, the studio acid-etched zebra motifs on slabs of 0.8mm-thick A5-sized brass plates that were subsequently hand-delivered to guests. The reverse side of the 'card' was also polished to a highly-reflective sheen to embody the event theme, appeal to the affluent attendees, and make a memorable impression. Similarly, Anagrama Studio utilised silver in designing eye-catching packaging for Neat Confections' handmade cookies and pastries on page 210. Although it is not-too-unusual a choice of material for the contents, they wanted to reflect the pure, impeccable, and flawless way with which the clients prepare each and every cookie, resulting in a fresh yet elegant visual identity embodying perfection.

In pushing the envelope, some artists and designers use gold and silver to add meaningful twists to original connotations and redefine the way people see things. For 'This Is Not Europe', Fons Hickmann used gold to mimic the spray paint effect of graffiti and reflect the confrontational nature of the event theme on page 414. By combining shiny splatters with the stoic black-and-white backdrop, he merged a serious topic with influences of everyday street art in a thoughtful way. On page 406, Panos Tsagaris' photographic work aims to transcend traditional practices of imagery by incorporating existing published material with transformative processes. The smooth, fragile, and appeasing surface of the gold leaf in his 'Golden Newspaper' series subverts the violence and intensity of the visual imagery on the base and at the same time, examines the questionable relationship between self and material wealth.

No matter how the palette is applied, gold and silver are timeless finishes and materials that make for undeniably striking outcomes. Ultimately, the onus lies on the artist or designer to ensure that they do not overpower the intended message.

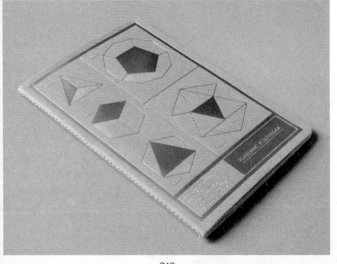

Silver.

Client
Deadly Ponies

Entry
Deadly Ponies Website

Consensus Spatial
Andrew Te'Aukoafa MNZ

Best.

Bronze.

Designers Institute of New Zealand
Best Design Awards 2011

Design Discipline
Interactive

Award Category
Large Scale Websites

Company
Alt Group

Design Director
Dean Poole

Design Team
Kris Lane, Nadia Alfonso

Client
Fisher & Paykel

Entry
Fisher & Paykel - Our Kitchen blog

Contributors
Fisher & Paykel

Consensus Graphic
Fraser Gardyne MNZ

Consensus Interactive
Che Tamahori

Consensus Product
Tony Parker MNZ

Consensus Spatial
Andrew Te'Aukoafa MNZ

cheers

10
9 8
7
6

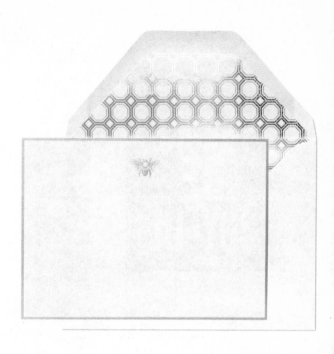

GIVE
THANKS
BE
JOYFUL

A TOAST TO YOU.

>>>———————→

Verena Michelitsch
Graphic Design & Illustration

+(43) 664 37 72 256
hello.verena@gmail.com
www.verenamichelitsch.com

Nice to meet you!

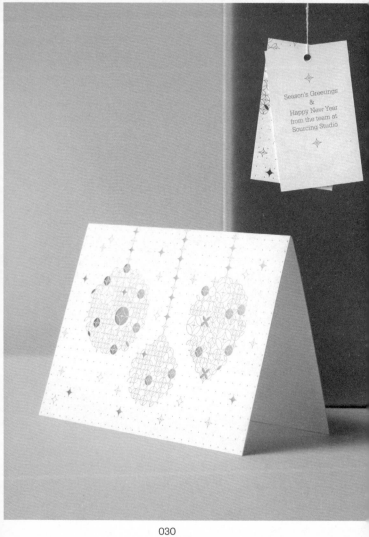

Season's Greetings
&
Happy New Year
from the team at
Sourcing Studio

Sourcing Studio

DATE
STYLE NO.
SAMPLE
SIZE
CUSTOMER
RANGE
FABRIC / YARN

APPROVAL

WWW.SOURCINGSTUDIO.COM

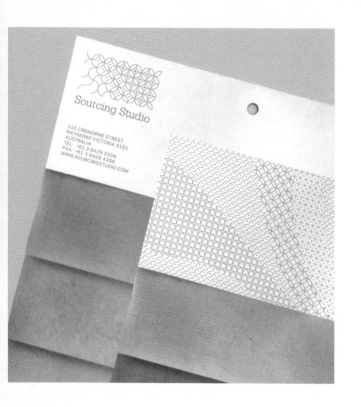

Sourcing Studio

115 CREMORNE STREET
RICHMOND VICTORIA 3121
AUSTRALIA
TEL. +61 3 9429 0356
FAX. +61 3 9429 4356
WWW.SOURCINGSTUDIO.COM

SHARON TAYLOR
DIRECTOR
—

SHARON@SOURCINGSTUDIO.COM.AU
WWW.SOURCINGSTUDIO.COM

MELBOURNE
115 CREMORNE STREET
RICHMOND VICTORIA 3121
AUSTRALIA
TEL: +61 3 9429 0356
FAX: +61 3 9429 4356
MOBILE: +61 411 457 272

SHANGHAI
#46 VIZCAYA
LANE 2000 YUN SHAN RD
JIN QIAO, PUDONG
SHANGHAI, 201206, P.R. CHINA
CELL: +86 13611 604 705

Sourcing Studio

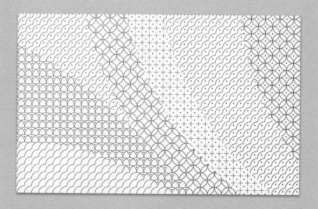

Carrer Alegre de Dalt 55
Primero, puerta A
Barcelona 08003

T +34 932 103 249
info@losiento.net
www.losiento.net

LO SIENTO

+34 932 103 249
M +34 615 125 604
rocio@losiento.net
www.losiento.net

4 Brompton Road
don SW3 2AS
ed Kingdom

☎ +44 (0)20 7225 1212
🖨 +44 (0)20 7225 1050
@ info@the-collection.co.uk
💻 www.the-collection.co.uk
www.the-collection.co.uk

Registered Of
London SW1 SAP
Registered in
VAT Num.

The owners of The Collection have
combined their passion for food
with their Mediterranean background
to create dishes that pay homage to
the very best produce of the "olive
oil" countries of southern Europe.
Being only olive oil in the cooking,
instead of butter, the dishes are
fresh and light.

The Collection is dedicated to using
only the finest ingredients
from suppliers such as the
Laverstoke Park and premi
butchers, O'Shea's of Kni
The menu offers sma
light bites, as well
and succulent
the grill.

the collection

the collection

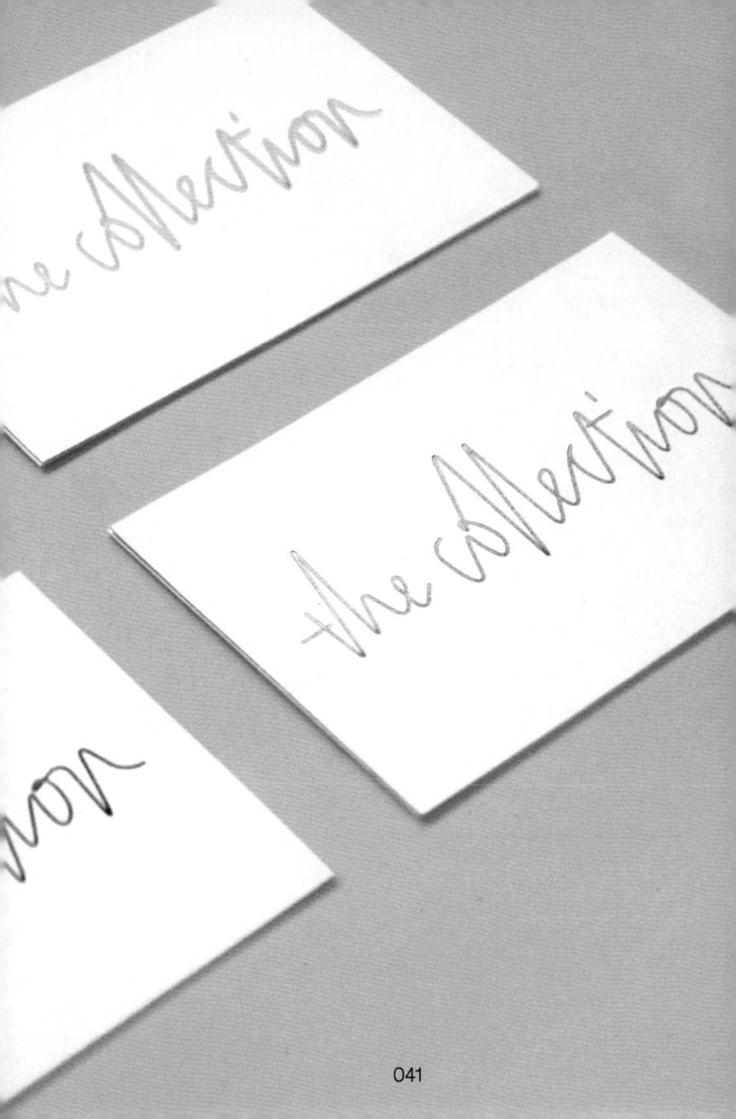
the collection

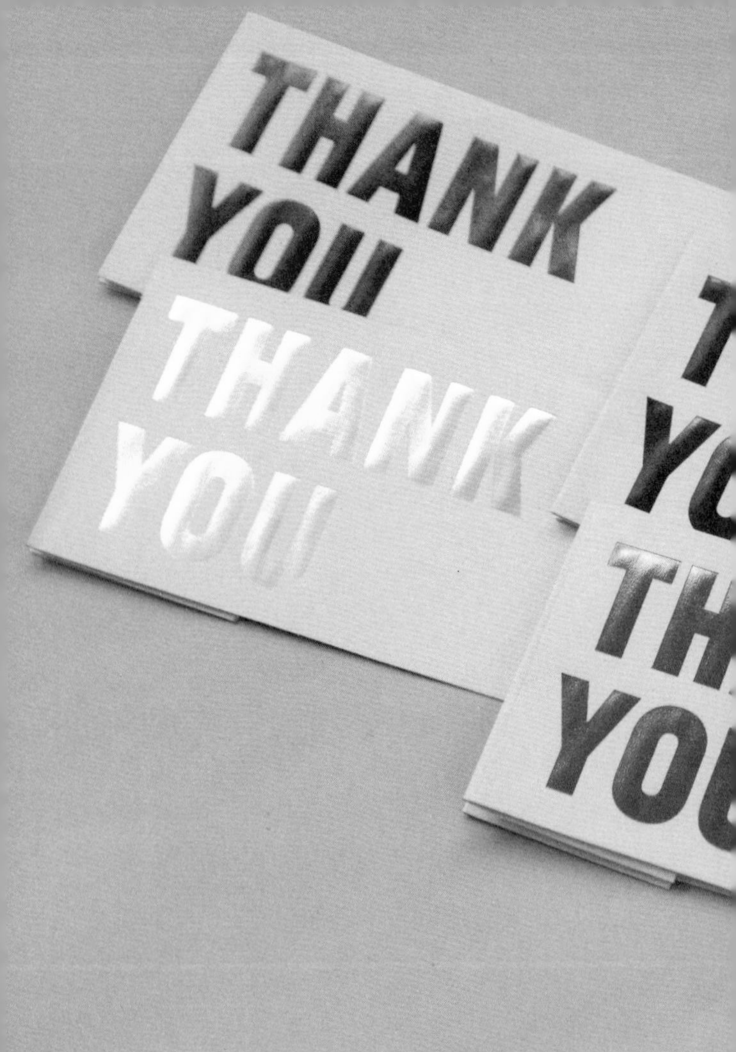
THANK YOU
THANK YOU

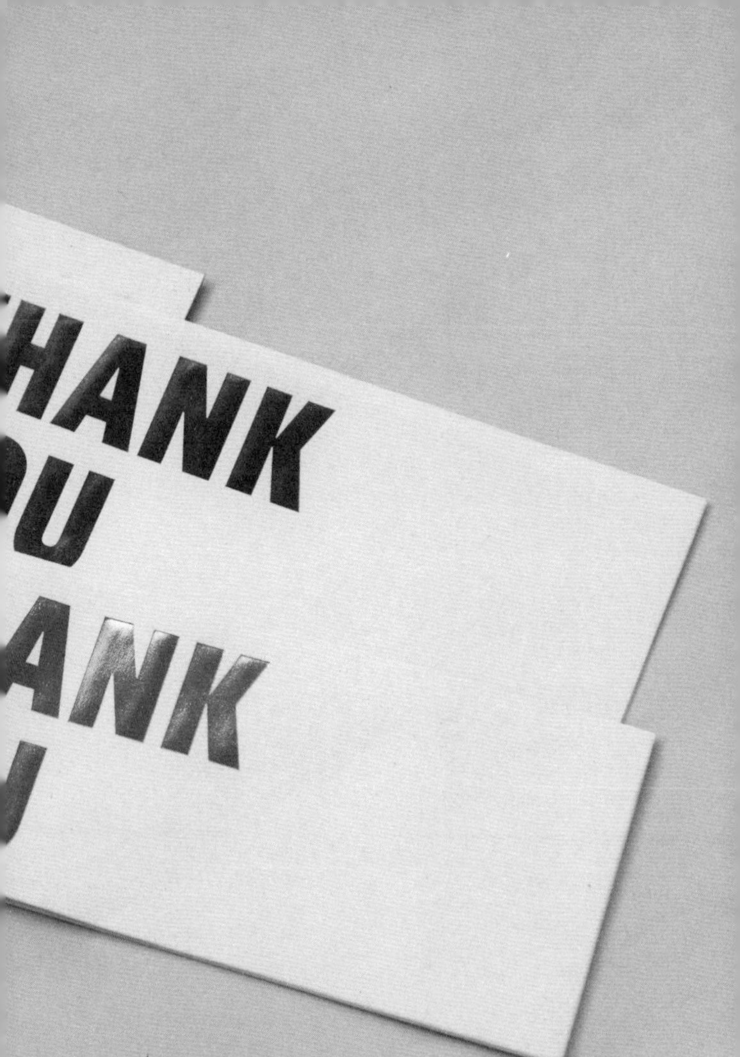
HANK
ANK

049

COCOA BUTTER, MILK, SUGAR,
CARAMEL CHUNKS, COOKIES

90's WHITE   ORIGIN: BRAZIL

BEST BEFORE JAN 2019

ILK SUGAR,

ORIGIN PERU

BEFORE JAN 2019

EVERYBODY NEEDS SEROTONIN

BE HAPPY!

01
MARSHMALLOWS & NUTS

110 gr

cokoa

"Metallics can be the protagonist in design. They are irreplaceable, not with any simple solid colour."

TRICOLETTE

TRICOLETTE YARNS
28 Primrose Road
Sheen's Wood
London NW8 ORG
020 7622 4044
yarns@tricoletteyarns.com
colletteyarns.com

TRICOLETTE

TRICOLETTE YARNS
93 Boundary Road
Off Abbey Road
St. John's Wood
London NW8 0RG

020 7372 4944
lynn@tricoletteyarns.com
tricoletteyarns.com

TRICOLETTE

TRICOLETTE YARNS
93 Boundary Road
Off Abbey Road
St. John's Wood
London NW8 0RG

020 7372 4944
lynn@tricoletteyarns.com
tricoletteyarns.com

1995 – 2005
/
10 ΧΡΟΝΙΑ
ΤΜΗΜΑ ΑΡΧΙΤΕΚΤΟΝΩΝ ΜΗΧΑΝΙΚΩΝ
ΠΑΝΕΠΙΣΤΗΜΙΟ ΠΑΤΡΩΝ

Πανεπιστημιούπολη, 265 00 Ρίο, Πάτρα
T. 2610 997 222, F. 2610 994 377
E. architect@upatras.gr, www.arch.upatras.gr

1995 – 2005
/
10 YEARS
DEPARTMENT OF ARCHITECTURE
UNIVERSITY OF PATRAS

University campus 265 00 Rion, Patras, Greece
T. +30 2610 997 552, F. +30 2610 969 377
E. architect@upatras.gr, www.arch.upatras.gr

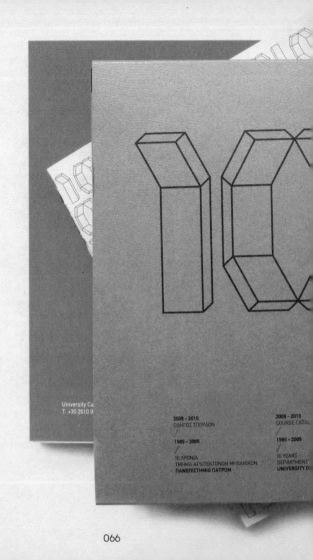

University Ca
T. +30 2610 9

2009 – 2010
ΟΔΗΓΟΣ ΣΠΟΥΔΩΝ

1999 – 2005

10 ΧΡΟΝΙΑ
ΤΜΗΜΑ ΑΡΧΙΤΕΚΤΟΝΩΝ ΜΗΧΑΝΙΚΩΝ
ΠΑΝΕΠΙΣΤΗΜΙΟ ΠΑΤΡΩΝ

2009 – 2010
COURSE CATAL

1999 – 2009

10 YEARS
DEPARTMENT
UNIVERSITY O

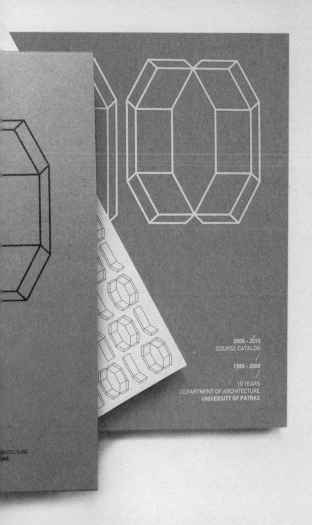

2009 – 2010
COURSE CATALOG

1999 – 2009

10 YEARS
DEPARTMENT OF ARCHITECTURE
UNIVERSITY OF PATRAS

RCHITECTURE
AS

nevertheless

a magazine for places / spaces / art / work
people / projects / reading / writing / fashion
design / photo / graphic / illustration

02

nevertheless

a magazine for places / spaces, art and
people / projects / relaxing / eating / love
design / photo / graphic / fashion

02

The iconic Liberty store will be transformed into a luxurious advent calendar revealing the most unique, captivating and glamorous of gifts.

———

For a sparkling festive season, step inside the enchanting splendour of the Liberty Tudor Building.

———

CHRISTMAS IN JULY 2008 PRESS PRE...
Tuesday 22nd July, 10am – 3pm, East Atr...

LIBERTY

LIBERTY

IN JULY 2008 PRESS PREVIEW AT **LIBERTY**
2nd July, 10am – 3pm, East Atrium Gallery, 4th Floor

AT **LIBERTY**
ery, 4th Floor

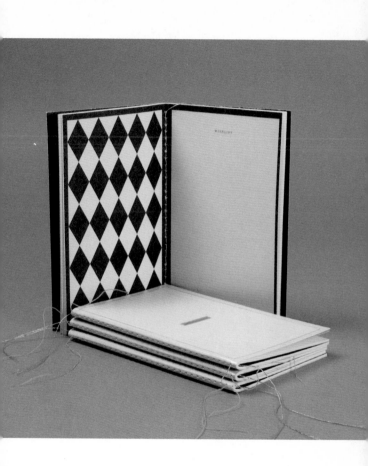

088

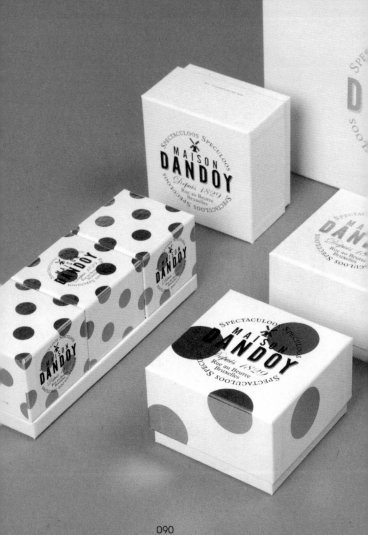

SPECTACULOOS SPECULOOS
MAISON
DANDOY
Depuis 1829
Rue au Beurre
Bruxelles
SPECTACULOOS

093

Artisanal biscuit
for frivolous mind.

Boterstraat 31 rue au Beurre
Brussel 1000 Bruxelles
Belgïe, Belgique

Tel: 32 (0)2 511.03.26
Fax: 32 (0)2 511.81.79

www.maisondandoy.com

MAISON DANDOY - 04/05   TVA-BTW: BE 0443 923 105   IBAN: 310 0144854 21   CBC: 191 0421160 36
                                                                 IBAN: BE70 3101 4485 8421   IBAN: BE61 1910 4211 6036
                                                                 BIC: BBRUBEBB   BIC: CREGBEBB

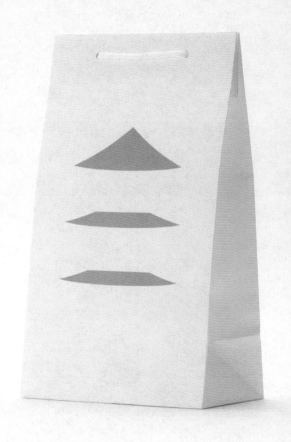

椿

歴史

世起口
上水陽
たを戌倉
桂吉

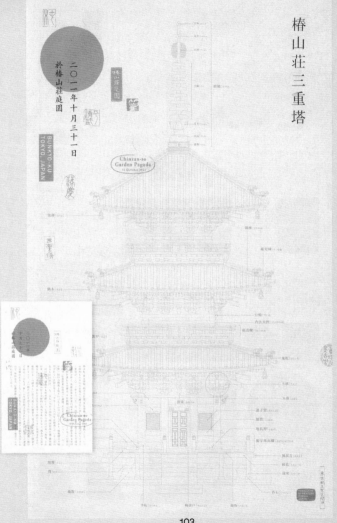

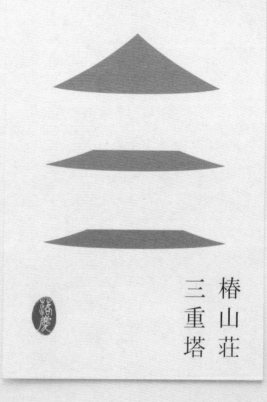

椿山荘
三重塔

BUNKYŌ-KU
TOKYO, JAPAN

椿山荘庭園

二〇二一年
十月三十一日
於椿山荘庭園

春は桜。夏は深緑。秋は月紅葉。冬は雪椿。いつ
の時代も人々の心を捉えて離さない美しい景色を紡ぎ出してきた
三重塔が、二〇二一年十月三十一日、百年の歳月を経て、称される平成の

修を終え、落慶法要を無事円成する。登録有形文化財
名を連ねる本塔は、平安前期、小野八）が慈山
竹林寺（広島県東広島市）に創建。また平安中期（一六〜一一八）
が第一回目の修復を執り行ったとの言い伝えがあり、建築様式や使
用されている材を見ると、少なくとも六百年は経過していると言わ
れるものである。一九二五（大正十四）年、関西財界の雄・藤田組
二代目社長、藤山雷太郎男爵によって現在の目白の杜へ移築。それ
以来、東京大空襲の折も奇跡的に消失を免れるなど、幾多の天災や
戦火をくぐり抜け、訪れる人々を見守り続けてきた本塔であるが、
後世にもこの雄々しい姿を、美しい風景を、受け継いで永く使命を
果たすべく、この晴れの日を迎えられたことは何よりも喜ばしい歓び
である。この札は、新しい生命が吹き込まれた本塔が庭災との遭遇
に見舞われることなく、百年先もこの地に立ち続ける願を込めたも
ので、無病息災、厄難退散を末永く保存していただ
ければ幸いである。

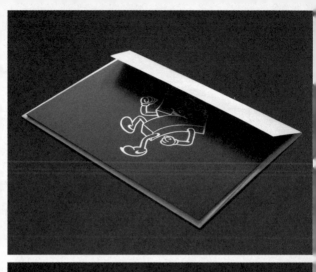

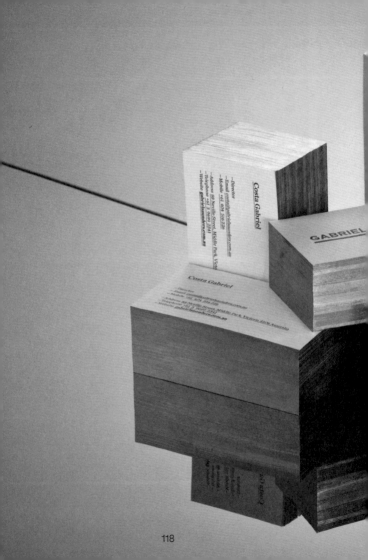

GABRIEL SAU

GABRIEL SAUNDERS

2011
Capabilities Document

SLICE | SINGAPORE

xstrata
coal

Creneau International
Atmosphere Architects

HEAD OFFICE

DUBAI

SYDNEY

PRAGUE

JAKARTA

KIEV

We hate to break it to you,
But today is a fickle thing
One day it's new, the next day it's gone
So in times like these,
Place your trust in what you know
And keep faith in what you trust.

Enjoy to work with you in 2010!

HAPPY HOLIDAYS &
A CREATIVE NEW YEAR

SERVICE INDUSTRIES

AVL Woningbouw, BERINGEN, BELGIUM / Fortis Northlight, BRUSSELS, BELGIUM / Proud Wilwey Joburg, Waste, BELGIUM
Infraz, HASSELT, BELGIUM / King Sturge EFQM, WOLvret, BELGIUM / Brewghor, WATERINA, BELGIUM

GRAPHICS & POS

..fe, Showbooks, WORLDWIDE / Belgian Beer Cafe, Identity, WORLDWIDE / Belharia Bin, Mo High, Opening event, BELGIUM
..l Lambert, Identity & Packaging & POS, WORLDWIDE / Vhats, POS & Packaging WORLDWIDE
..mfly, GENK, BELGIUM

In&Out
Masayoshi Nakajo

饮
伸
&
禁
正
呕

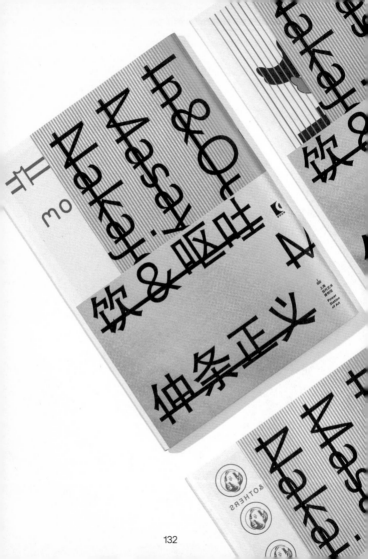

"The metallic foil and matt paper are designed to feel good in the hand, look good on the shelf, and evoke the taste of the Jazz Age, the base of Fitzgerald's stories."

F. SCOTT FITZGERALD FLAPPERS AND PHILOSOPHERS

F. SCOTT FITZGERALD THE BEAUTIFUL AND DAMNED

F. SCOTT FITZGERALD THE LAST TYCOON

F. SCOTT FITZGERALD THE GREAT GATSBY

F. SCOTT FITZGERALD TENDER IS THE NIGHT

F. SCOTT FITZGERALD THIS SIDE OF PARADISE

PENGUIN CLASSICS

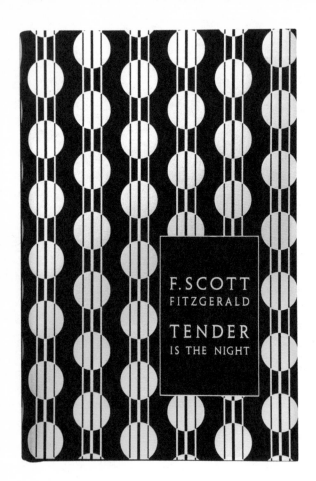

F. SCOTT
FITZGERALD

TENDER
IS THE NIGHT

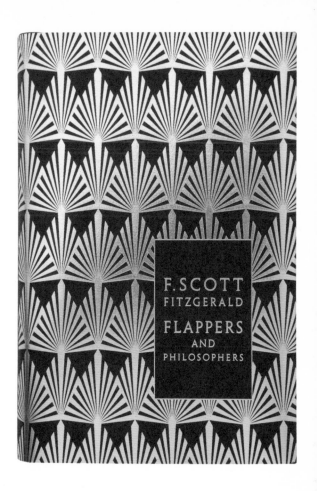

F. SCOTT
FITZGERALD

FLAPPERS
AND
PHILOSOPHERS

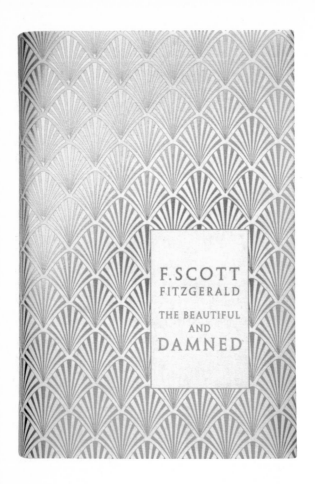

F. SCOTT
FITZGERALD

THE BEAUTIFUL
AND
DAMNED

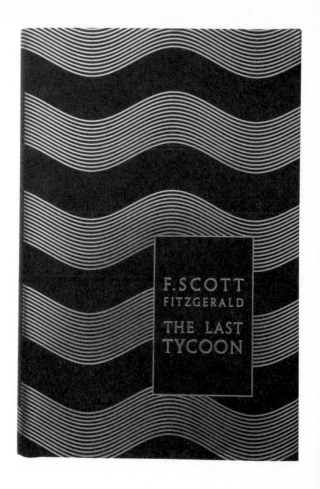

F.SCOTT
FITZGERALD

THE LAST
TYCOON

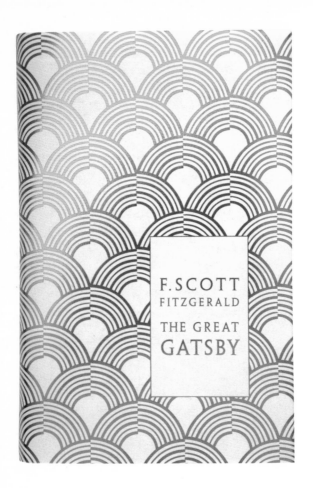

F. SCOTT
FITZGERALD

THE GREAT
GATSBY

F. SCOTT
FITZGERALD

THIS SIDE OF
PARADISE

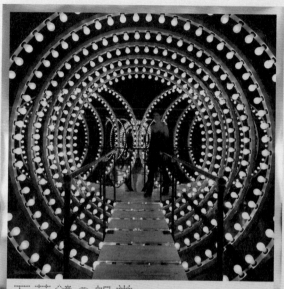

森美術館 六本木ヒルズ森タワー53階　2009年4月4日[土]-7月5日[日]

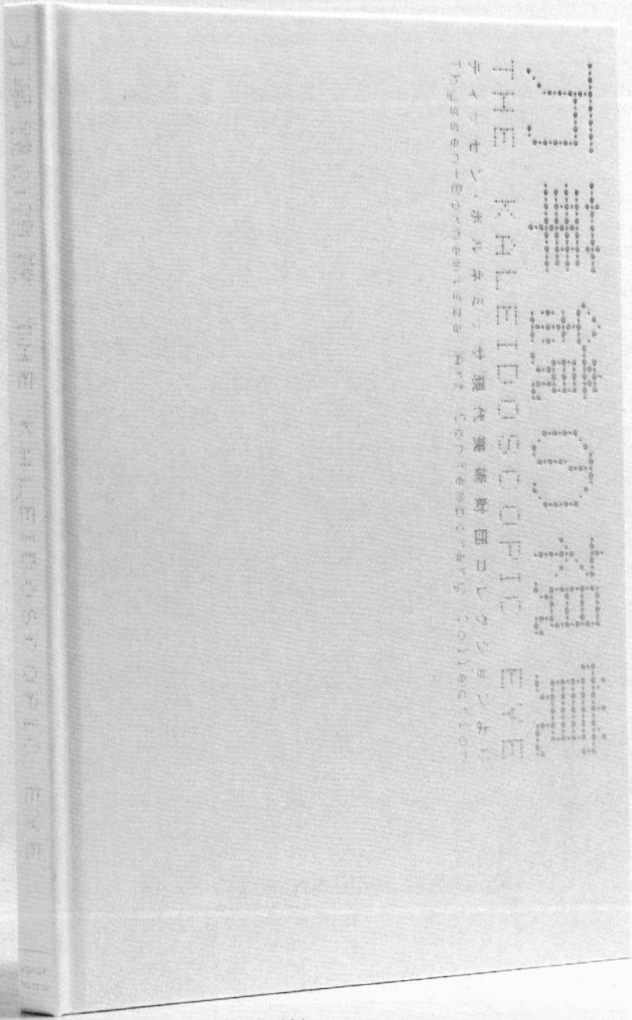

万華鏡の視覚

THE KALEIDOSCOPIC EYE

ティッセン＝ボルネミッサ現代美術コレクションより
Thyssen-Bornemisza Art Contemporary Collection

145

万華鏡の視覚
THE KALEIDOSCOPIC EYE
ティッセン―ボルネミッサ現代美術財団コレクションより
Thyssen-Bornemisza Art Contemporary Collection

森美術館
主催：森美術館
協賛：パナソニック電工株式会社

Mori Art Museum
Organized by: Mori Art Museum
Institutional Support: Thyssen-Bornemisza Art Contemporary
Support: Austrian Embassy

六本木ヒルズ森タワー53階　2009年4月4日[土]―
ティッセン―ボルネミッサ現代美術財団　後援：オーストリア大使館
協力：日本航空、ニコラ・フィアット、株式会社音響総合研

Roppongi Hills Mori Tower　4 April–5 July, 2009
Thyssen-Bornemisza Art Contemporary
Japan Embassy　Corporate Sponsor: Panasonic Electric Works Co.,
Nicolas Feuillatte; Acoustic Technical Laboratory

MORI ART MUSEUM

[roppongi hills]

Mori Art Museum, Thyssen-Bornemisza Art Contemporary
Sponsor: Austrian Embassy　Corporate
Japan Airlines, Nicolas Feuillatte; Acoustic Technical

MORI ART MUSEUM

[roppongi hills]

目を奪う、心揺さぶる
ートに出会う

を奪う、心揺さぶる、
ートに出会う

割引券　DISCOUNT

一般　ADULT
¥1,500→¥1,300(税込)

学生　STUDENT
¥1,000→¥900(税込)

本券提示により5名様まで有効
Valid for up to
5 people

Thyssen-Bornemisza
Art Contemporary

WWW.MORI ART MUSEUM

日[日]

万華鏡の視覚

THE KALEIDOSCOPIC EYE

ティッセン・ボルネミッサ現代美術財団コレクションより
Thyssen-Bornemisza Art Contemporary Collection

森美術館 六本木ヒルズ森タワー53階 **2009年4月4日[土]−7月5日[日]**
Mori Art Museum 53F Roppongi Hills Mori Tower 4 April-5 July, 2009

2009年4月3日[金]
内覧会 17:00−19:30 レセプション 18:00−19:30 [最終受付:19:00]
Date: Friday, 3 April, 2009 Exhibition Preview: 17:00-19:30
Opening Reception: 18:00-19:30 (register by 19:00)

MORI ART MUSEUM

Thyssen-Bornemisza
Art Contemporary

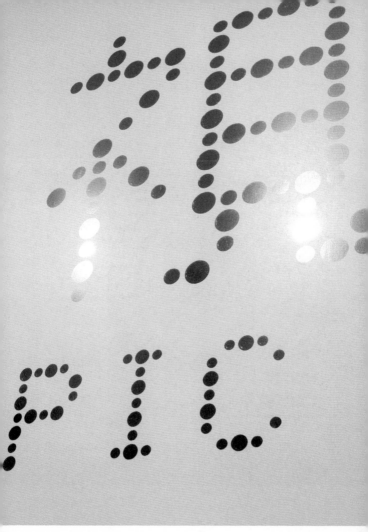

Berliner Zimmer

Sarajevo

Warhol
sobre
Warhol
on
Warhol
sobre
Warhol
on
Warhol
sobre
Warhol
on
Warhol
sobre
Warhol
on
Warhol
sobre
Warhol
on
Warhol
sobre
Warhol
on
Warhol
sobre
Warhol
on
Warhol

La Casa
Encendida

23.11.2007 > 20.01.2008

Warhol
on
Warhol
sobre
Warhol
on
Warhol
sobre
Warhol
on
Warhol
sobre
Warhol
on
W...
so...
W...
on
W...
so...
W...hol
on
...arhol
...bre
...arhol

...arhol
...bre
Warhol
on
Warhol
sobre
Warhol
on
Warhol

La Casa
Encendida

23.11.2007 > 20.01.2008

159

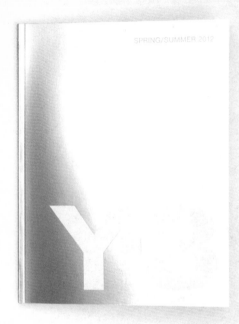

SPRING/SUMMER 2012

28
Y-3 SPR

Y-3

INVITES YOU TO CELEBRATE
ITS FIVE YEAR ANNIVERSARY
WITH THE OPENING OF
THE FIRST PARIS STORE.

THURSDAY OCTOBER 4ᵀᴴ AT 20H30

Y-3
12 ETIENNE MARCEL
001 PARIS

R.S.V.P. BY OCTOBER 1ˢᵀ 2007
T +33 (0)1 420 15100
Y-3@PRESSINGONLINE.COM

Y-3
INVITES YOU TO CELEBRATE
ITS FIVE YEAR ANNIVERSARY
WITH THE OPENING OF
THE FIRST PARIS STORE.

DAY OCTOBER 4TH AT 20H30

NE MARCEL

170

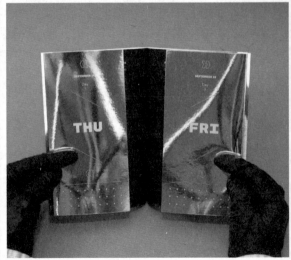

178

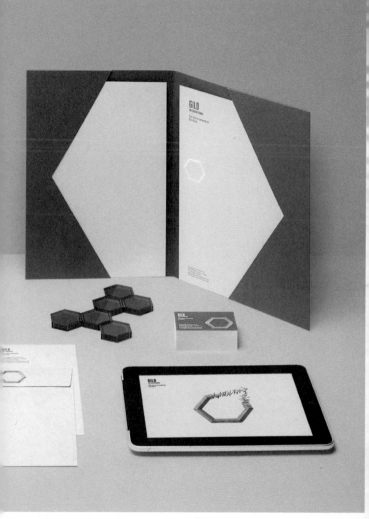

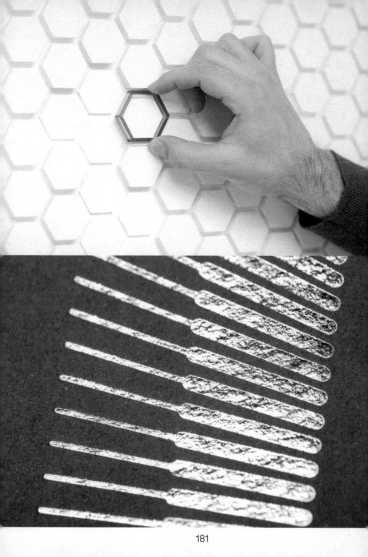

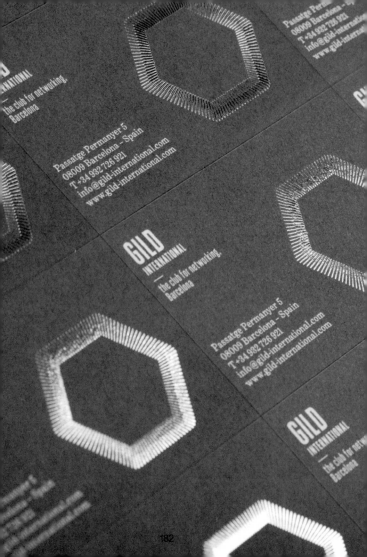

trash can

mintdesigns

017 .21 Tue
- 3.25 Sat
11:00-19:00

Graphic &
Textile
Works

at Creation Gallery G8

2001   2017

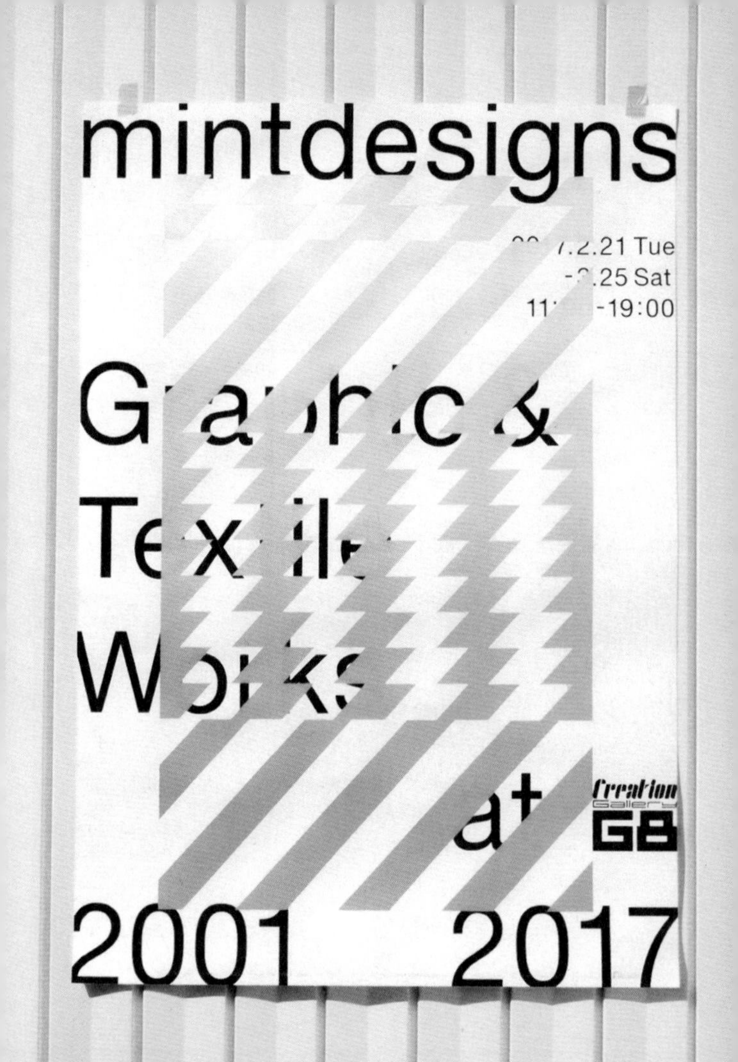

mintdesigns

2017.2.21 Tue
-2.25 Sat
11:00-19:00

Graphic &
Textile
Works

at

Creation
Gallery
G8

2001   2017

mintdesigns

2001.2.21 Tue
-3.25 Sat
11:00-19:00

Graphic &
Textile
Works

"Graphic & Textile Works 2001-2017" mir

2001   2017

190

PHARMACY

PLACE

placebopharmacy.eu

An iconic presence,
a place devoted to human nature.
Providing a new mindset for the word
'pharmacy', promoting a positive
attitude and wellbeing,
filling your days with happiness.
Above all, 'placebo' derives
from the Latin 'I will please'.

Positive Thoughts.
Everyday.

A gift is always positive. →

21   Changed your mind?

5

← Return within 15 days

PHARMACY

PLACI

"The opaque and reflective behaviours of metallic inks help bring depth and diversity to our printed materials."

First
Floor
Financial
Engineering

First
Floor
Finan
Eng

or
nancial
ngineering

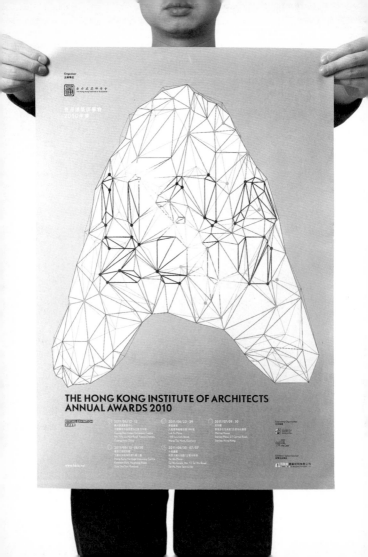

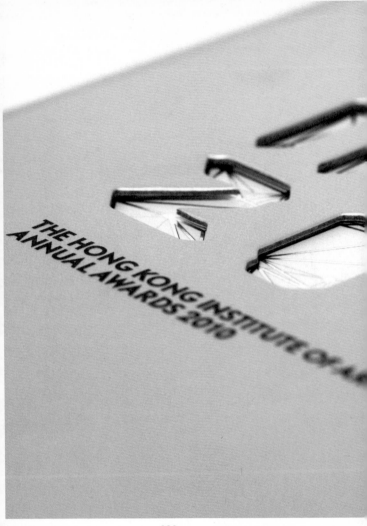

THE HONG KONG INSTITUTE OF AR
ANNUAL AWARDS 2010

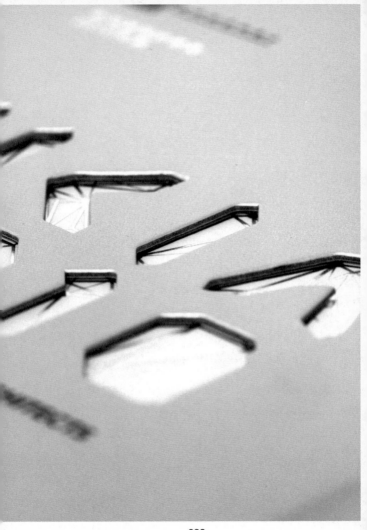

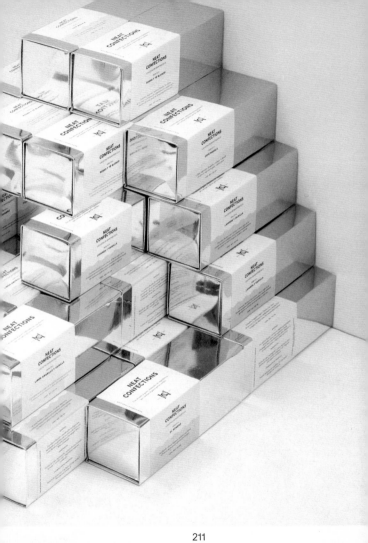

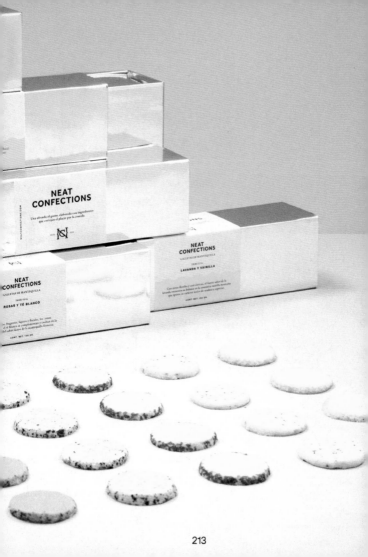

213

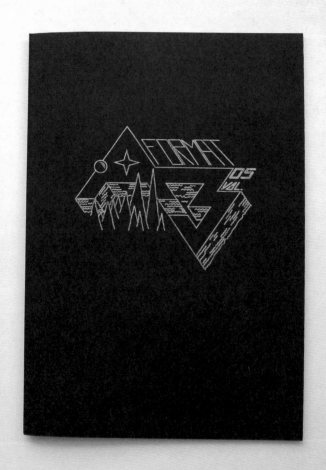

Дете - "Деца су мали људи, могу бити добри и мање добри."
A child - "Children are little people, they can be good and less good."

ШЈАВОРРО
ШЈАВОРРЕ СИ ЦИКНЕ МАНУША, ШАЈ АВЕН ЛАЧХЕ ТХАЈ МАЈЦАРРА ЛАЧХЕ

a3format.org
Ana Bojanović - Belgrade

220

Бршîнд - Чи волив бршîнд, кана пере
царе
Иван Петрушевски / Ivan Petruševski
www.behance.net/fimovski
Ненад Поњевић / Nenad Ponjević
www.behance.net/NenadPonjevic
ЊAMO
Весна Пешић / Vesna Pešić
www.becha.me
www.behance.net/BECHA
Јурij Лозић / Jurij Lozić
www.zek.si
Ива Спасојевић / Iva Spasojević
www.ivaspasojevic.com
www.flickr.com/photos/zebrumera
Нина Зељковић / Nina Zeljković
www.flickr.com/photos/traum
Маријана Зарић / Marijana Zarić
Супер Тимор / Super Timor
Mina Fina

PARFUMEUR
FLORES

PRVI
ROĐENDAN
INSTITUT
PARFUMEUR
FLORES
SUBOTA
28.11.2009

www.flores-group.com

INSTITUT
PARFUMEUR
FLORES

PRVI
ROĐENDAN
INSTITUT
PARFUMEUR
FLORES
SUBOTA
28.11.2009

www.flores-group.com

FINE GOLD 9999

THE INFINITE FUTURE

THE GOLDEN AGE IS BEFORE US, NOT BEHIND US.

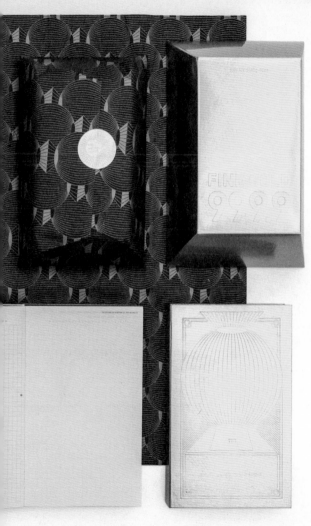

229

THE GOLDEN AGE
IS BEFORE US,
NOT BEHIND US.

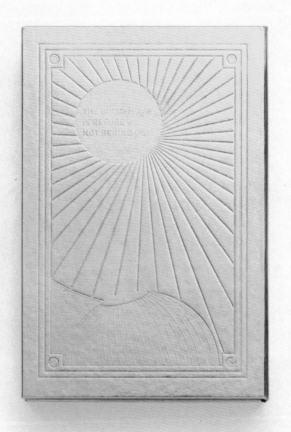

THE GOLDEN AGE
IS BEFORE US
NOT BEHIND US

NET WT 1000g-33oz

FINE GOLD

9999

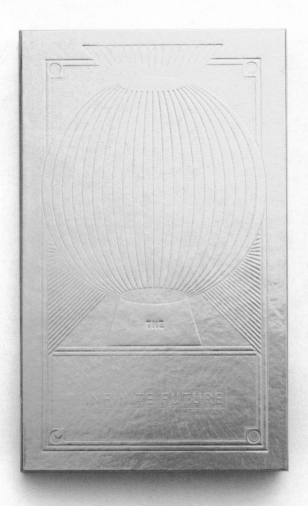

the

INFINITE FUTURE

SO EIN I
SIE AUC
FORESTIL DIG D
LØB MED TYSKI
SALG OG BUNDL
FOR DIN EKSPOI
DAFI, DM&T, DE OG DA
INVITERER TIL KONFE
BESLUTNINGER SOM I
KONFERENCEN GIVER DIG:
· UDFORDRING PÅ DIN EKSPORTSTR
· VIDEN OG INSPIRATION OM DET TY
· NYE RELATIONER TIL AKTØRER I T
TSCHÜSS

TYSK EKSPORT /
MARKEDSANALYSE
Demografi, kabelkraft, betalingsbetingelser
agentsamarbejde, messer

01

誠邀閣下出席雞尾酒會
預祝我們在「香港國際藝術展 10」
展出成功

日期：
2010年5月28日 (星期二) 晚上6時正

地點：
KEE CLUB
中環威靈頓街32號鏞記大廈6樓

敬請兩覆
請於2010年5月21日 (星期五)
或之前電郵至
LAUREN@CHANHARRIE.COM

PLEASE JOIN

AT OUR ARTHK 2010
PRE-OPENING PARTY

9PM TUESDAY 25 MAY

KEE CLUB

32 WELLINGTON ST
6TEH FLOOR CENTRAL

RSVP TO
LAUREN@GRANTPIRRIE.COM
BY FRIDAY 21 MAY

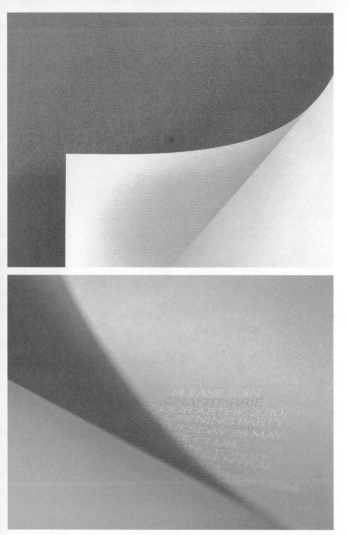

"Metallics bring a layer of depth and luxury that can really add to the personality of a brand."

255

MOON LANDING

21 July 1969 / 02:56:48 GMT
First step on the moon

(50) 1969 → 2019
MOON LANDING

NASA

NASA

NASA

Anicorn × Nasa
Lunar Sample Return
Collection

Limited to
300 units worldwide

(50) 1969→2019
MOON LANDING

Anicorn × Nasa
LUNAR SAMPLE RETURN Collection

21 July 1969 / 02 56 48 GMT

NASA

50ᵗʰ Anniversary of Moon Landing

The 50ᵗʰ Anniversary campaign of Moon
Landing marked a semi-centennial date of
human making history, it also kicks off the new
era for space exploration, some other agencies
are planning moon journeys for human in the
coming years.

To celebrate the half-century anniversary,
ANICORN Watches teamed up with NASA to
create a limited "LUNAR SAMPLE RETURN"
Collection. To tribute the effort made for moon
landing, and to acknowledge the importance of
the LUNAR-EARTH relationships.

(50) 1969→2019
MOON LANDING

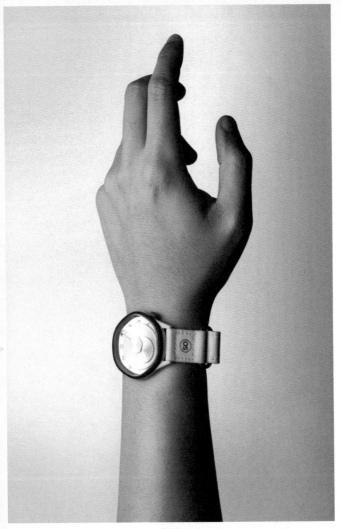

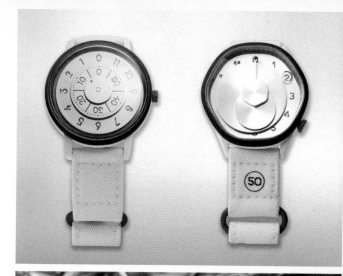

259

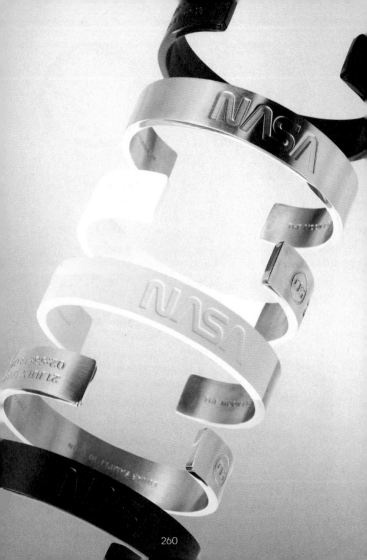

261

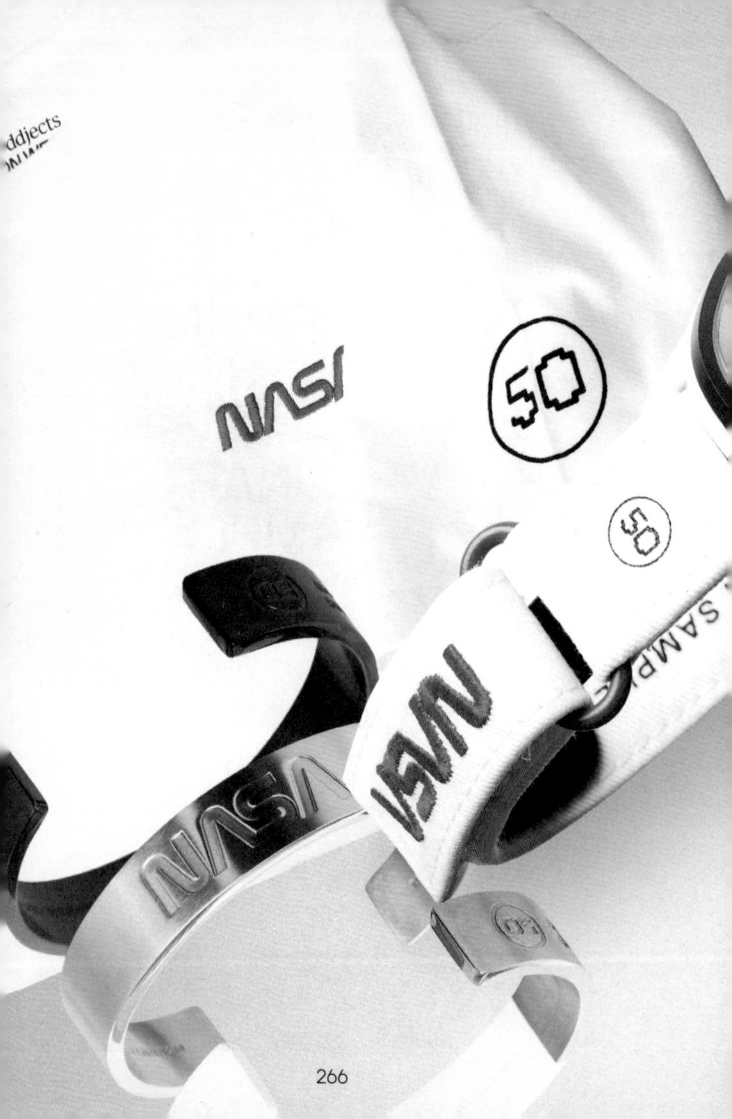
NASA
50

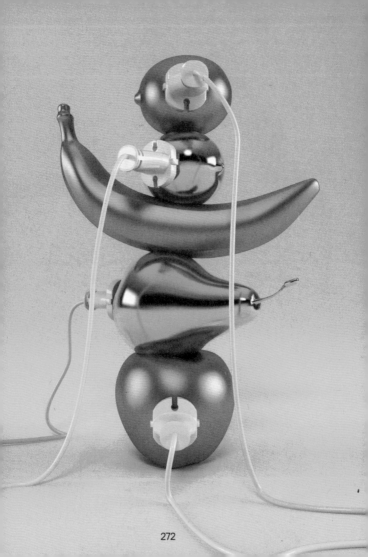

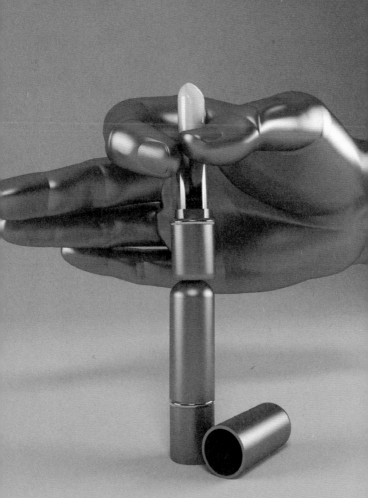

BAPE®ARCHIVES
BY NIGO®

ISBN978-4-9906316-0-4
C0176

PUBLISHED BY
honeyee.com

000108

Le 36 rue Beaujon vous
unique, des bureaux
de Paris. Depuis
nous avons
secteurs
intern

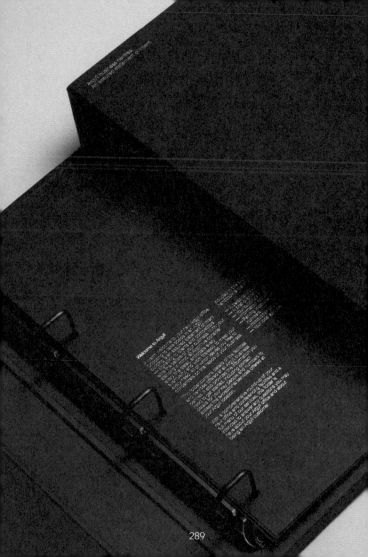

...in the...
...ed on one of...
...s, flanked by Rog...
...kingham Palace, this...
...listed building was a gi...
Charles II to Nell Gwynn an...
in history.
Please join us on Thursday 1...
-tember 2008, from 12:30-2:30pm...
champagne, canapés & a personal...
the beautifully designed in...
with a luxurious gift an...
Please RSVP to E...
Pall Mall, Londo...
emily.taylor@ec...
We look f...
Arg...

... Let...
...ur complim...
...y Taylor at 78
...W 1 Y 5 ES, or email
...oup.com.
...ard to welcoming you.
Yours Sincerely.
Emily Taylor

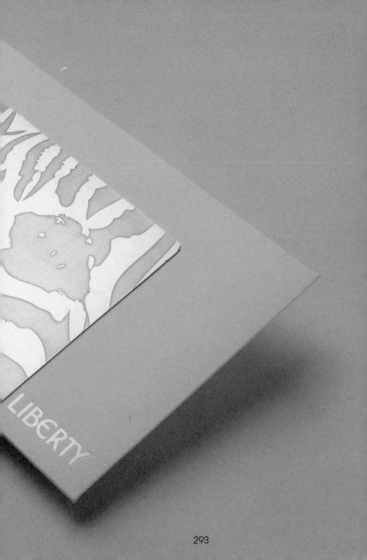

LIBERTY

Geoffroy de La Bourdonnaye

+

Yasmin Sewell

Have the pleasure of inviting you to an exclusive preview
of Liberty's fashion renaissance

Thursday 5th February
7 – 10 pm
(dinner at 8pm)

RSVP:
Kate Brindley
kbrindley@liberty.co.uk
0207 573 9431

LIBERTY

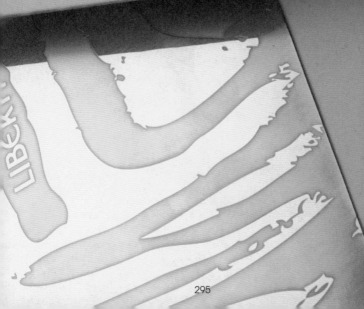

Ganz ganz weit oben
Mit Priorität AAA
der ToDo list des Vergessens
wir den Fluchtpunkt deiner
Wahrnehmung
groß ist wie das Saarland
er das bleibt unter uns

hwärzten Einbausatz
ner Wahrnehmung
ge ich mit einem
kappenbomber
Wahrnehmung
bt unter uns

rität AAA
gessens
er uns
ns!

Alles weiter in...
durch d...
Seme erzählt die um eine...
Irgendwo am anderen Ende dieses...
Sagt die...
Alles s...

Die Kinder ja ja die Kinder
Aus Epigonen am anderen Ende dieses Baums
Irgendwo am anderen Ende dieses Baums
Schreiben wir dir eine Ansichtskarte

IN SERIE

Ich habe mich - ich habe mich
Ich sehe mich schon
Sehe mich schon

Über zuviel kann ich zu wenig sagen
Wir unterhalten uns
In Serie in Serien in Serie
Nicht zu politisch nicht vor dem
man Angst haben muss
Wir unterhalten uns
Unterhalten uns

Über zuviel kann ich zu wenig sagen
Wir unterhalten uns
In Serie in Serien in Serie
Nicht zu politisch nichts vor dem
man Angst haben muss

In Serie in Serie
Und mit schrecken halten wir Angst
in Serie
Unterhalte uns

Mit Stimmen
Jede ein leuchtend und Gesichter
Ihr durch Wände gehen
Los uns durch Wände gehen
Los uns durch
Da sind durch

01
Weltmarktführer
02
Befehl von oben
03
Ansichtskarte
04
Erinnern
05
Aufmerksamkeit
06
In Serie
07
Polaroid
08
Sonstiges
09
Version
10
Machen
11
Die Aufständischen
12
Deutschland 001
13
Ziel

BROKENSILENCE

INITIATIVE
MUSIK

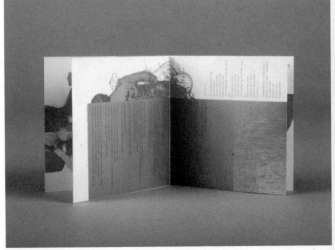

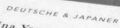

DEUTSCHE & JAPANER

Ina Yamaguchi
イナ ヤマグチ

+49 621 32674360
iy@deutscheundjapaner.com

Weylstraße 4
68167 Mannheim
Germany

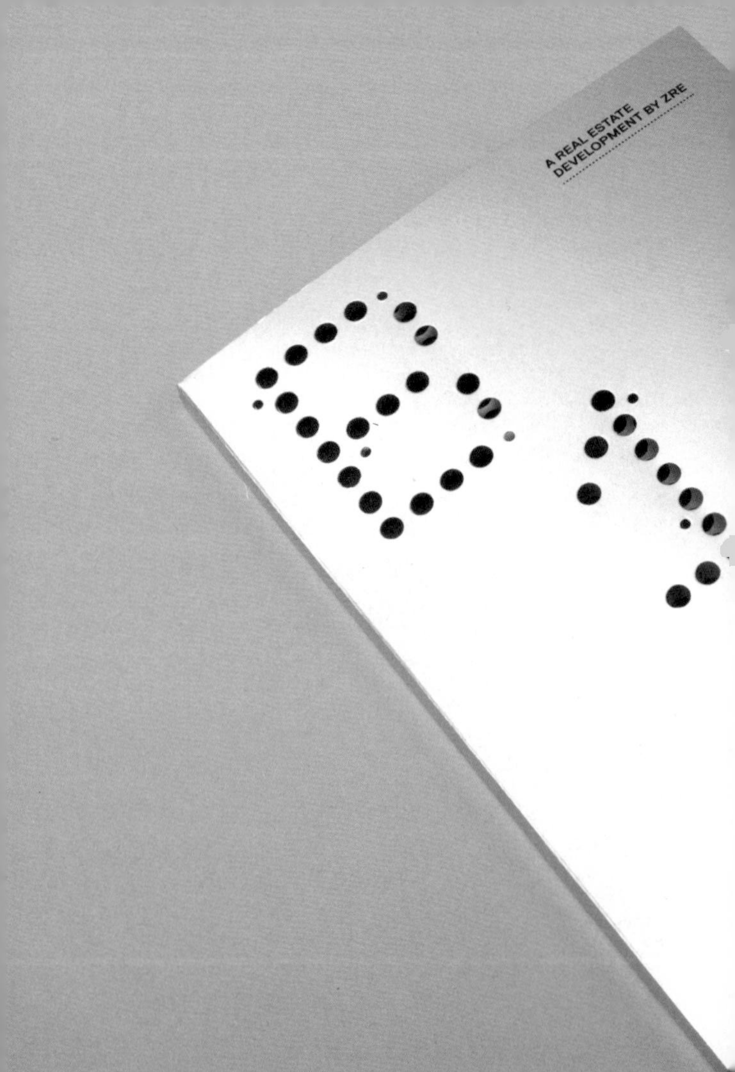
A REAL ESTATE
DEVELOPMENT BY ZRE

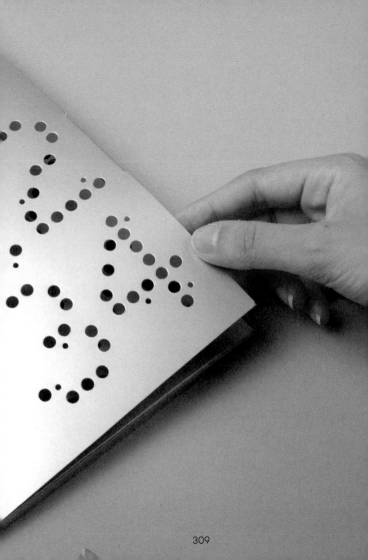

A REAL EST
DEVELO

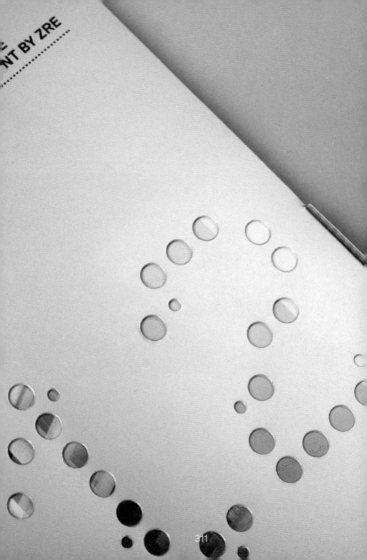

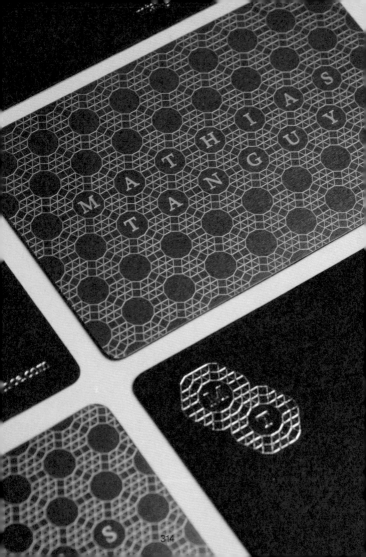

Mathias Tanguy
Fiscaliste
Cabinet Exell Finance
Ingénierie fiscale
06 68 40 03 11
mtanguy@exellfinance.com

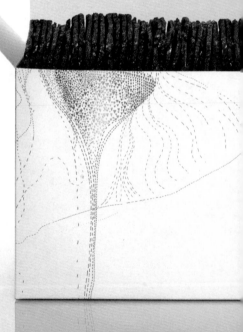

CATALINA FERNĀN

TALLER REPOSTERO

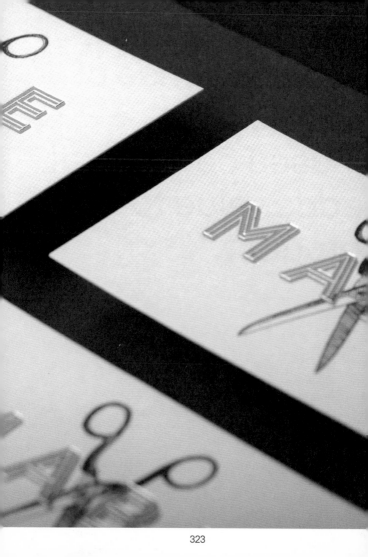

"It helps give a brand a sense of quality. And if used correctly, it adds value to the product."

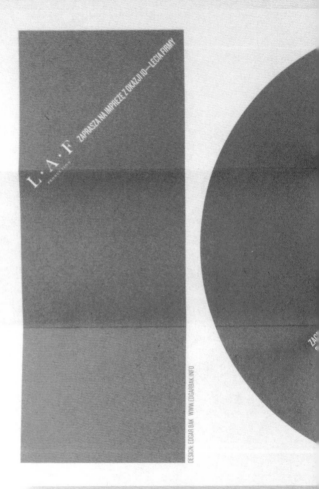

L·A·F ZAPRASZA NA IMPREZĘ Z OKAZJI 10—LECIA FIRMY

DESIGN: EDGAR BĄK WWW.EDGARBAK.INFO

KAPITAN SPARKY I ZESPÓŁ SAMBAL. PIĄTEK, 26 CZERWCA 2009 R. START O GODZINIE 21:00
...RZA, UL. RYDYGIERA 8 (WEJŚCIE OD ULICY BURAKOWSKIEJ), WARSZAWA
... MONIKA WAGNER, TEL. 0—503—056—806, EMAIL: M.WAGNER@LAF.COM.PL

GOLD RUSH

HKDA GLOBAL DESIGN AWARDS 2011

香港設計師協會 環球設計大獎 2011

CALL FOR ENTRIES
作品徵集

HKDA GLOBAL DESIGN AWARDS 2011 SINCE 1975

CATEGORIES AND JUDGES 參賽類別及評審團

GRAPHIC 平面

DUTCH
MICHEL DE BOER

NORWAY
KJELL EKHORN

UK
MICHAEL JOHNSON

SWEDEN
CARIN OLDHLM SVENSSON

HONG KONG
CHUNG MAN YEE

PRODUCT 產品

ITALY
LUISA BOCCHIETTO

FRANCE
MATALI CRASSET

FINLAND
HARRI KOSKINEN

SPATIAL 空間

UK
ADAM BRINKWORTH

JAPAN
MASAYUKI KUROKAWA

USA
HANI RASHID

NEW MEDIA 新媒體

JAPAN
KENTARO KATSUBE

HONG KONG
JEFFREY SHAW

CHINA
JOHAN VAKIDIS

2011 / 10 / 11

SUBMISSION DEADLINE 參賽報名截止日期

NO EXTENSION 絕不延期

www.hongkongda.com/awards2011

HKDA GLOBAL DESIGN AWARDS 2011
香港設計師協會 環球設計大獎 2011
—

IS COMING

CALL FOR ENTRIES SOON 作品徵集即將開始

www.hongkongda.com/awards2011

PRODUCT
產品

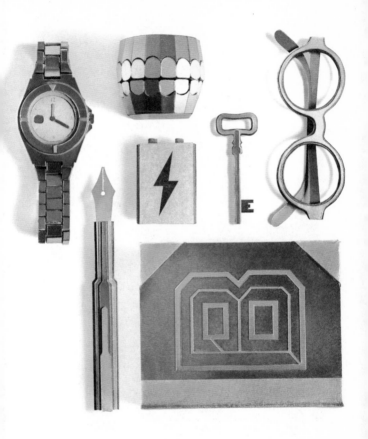

333

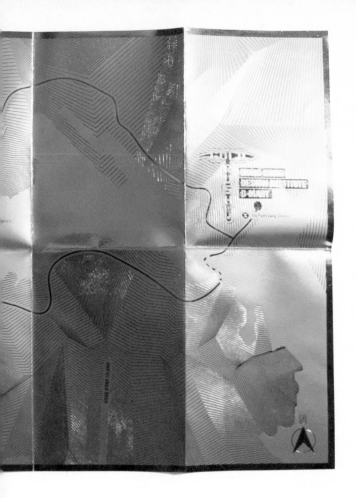

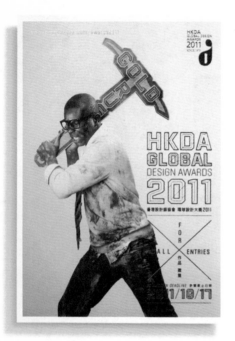

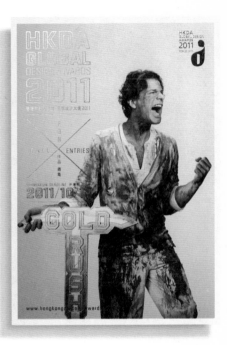

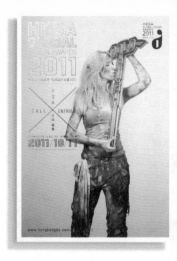

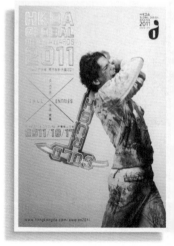

340

Jon Evans
Co-Founder
Creative Director—

—7 Printing House Yard
Shoreditch
London E2 7PR

+44 (0) 7790 147 033
+44 (0) 207 739 7244
jon@pennyroyal.tv
pennyroyal.tv

Printing House Yard
Shoreditch
London E2 7PR

under—
Director—

+44 (0) 7790 147 033
+44 (0) 207 739 7244
jon@pennyroyal.tv
pennyroyal.tv

Penny
Royal
Films

Penny Royal
3 Printing House Yard
Shoreditch
London E2 7PR
+44 (0) 207 729 7744
info@pennyroyal.tv
pennyroyal.tv

Penny Royal is a creative
led visual communication
studio housing a new wave
of experienced multi-
disciplinary Film Directors,
Animators and Designers.

From generating ideas
to executing them,
Penny Royal specialises
in a variety of creative
areas from Live Action,
CGI and Motion Graphics
to Interactive Design,
Sound Design, Branding
and Concept Development.

Penny
Royal
Films

© Copyright Notice
All copyrights and content
in this disc are property
owned by Penny Royal Films,
unless stated otherwise.
No third party may copy, use
or distribute this disc without
or any part of its without
express Penny Royal Films
from Penny Royal Films.

pennyroyal.tv

Here is some of our latest work.
Let us know what you think.

January
2012

Black Blacksmith

Virgin Media
This is our next promo for Virgin Media. It will be it's nationally broadcast over the nationwide brand on TV to advertise the new season of the Virgin Media drama, and a huge success and scooped several accolades as well as positive feedback from our client at Virgin Media.

OLYMPIC GAMES
LONDON 2012

OLYMPIC GAMES
LONDON 2012

GET IT, IF YOU WANT IT.

SINGULAR HOTEL

SINGULAR JOY

Calle Norte 16, Col C4 Mexico
Phone 044 Contacto 32, Resa, Mx

SINGULAR DREAM

Calle Durango 103, esq C7 161 Mx
Phone 044 Contacto 5, Resa, Mx

SINGULARHOTEL.MX

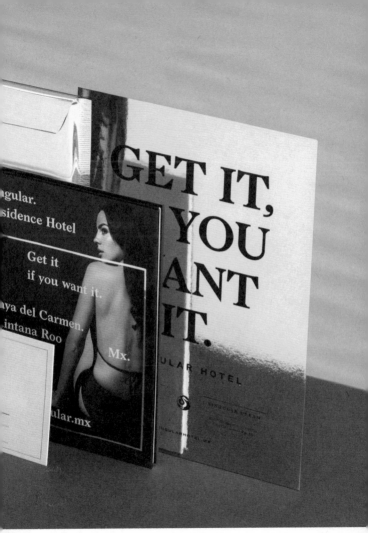

PLAYA DEL CARMEN, MEXICO

SINGULAR
HOTEL

SINGULAR JOY

Get it, if you want it.

SINGULAR DREAM

SINGULARHOTEL.MX

PLAYA DEL CARMEN, MEXICO

SINGULAR
HOTEL

SING...   — Get ...

355

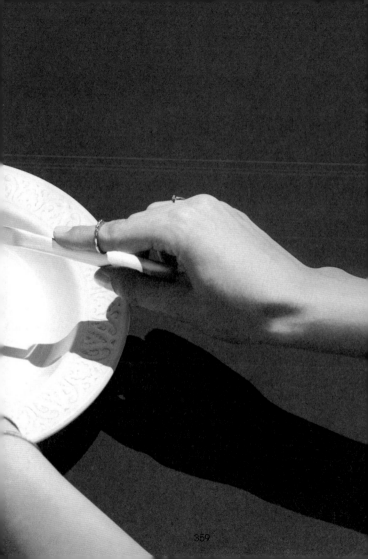

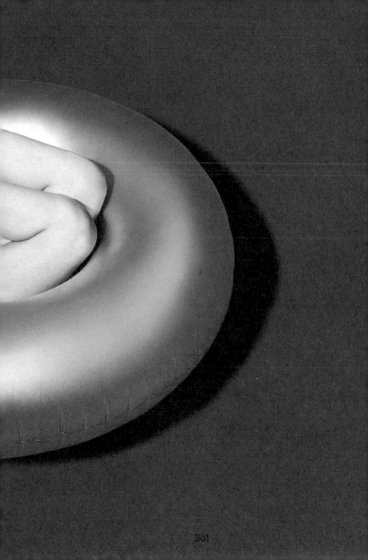

"Metallic colours look best when they have a reason to be there."

The Carriageworks
Screen Listings
Oscar Winners Month
Throughout February

Casablanca
The King's Speech
The Silence of the Lambs
Schindler's List
Dances with Wolves

The Carriageworks
Oscar Winners Month

Forrest Gump (1995)

Date	Time	Screen	Rating	Price
Mon 20th Feb	8:00pm	2	12	£3.50 Adult

The Carriageworks
Oscar Winners Month

Forrest Gump (1995)

Date   Time   Screen   Rating
Mon 20th Feb   8:00pm   2   12

The Carriageworks
Oscar Winners Month

The Sound of Music (1966)

Date	Time	Screen	Rating	Price
Tue 21st Feb	3:00pm	2	U	£2.50 Child

The Carriageworks
Oscar Winners Month

The Sound of Music (1966)

Date   Time   Screen   Rating
Tue 21st Feb   3:00pm   2   U

The Carriageworks
Oscar Winners Month

Gone with the Wind (1940)

Date	Time	Screen	Rating	Price
Tue 12th Feb	7:00pm	1	PG	£3.50 Adult

The Carriageworks
Oscar Winners Month

Gone with the Wind (1940)

Date   Time   Screen   Rating
Tue 12th Feb   7:00pm   1   PG

Monday

Tuesday

Wednesday

Thursday

Friday

1 Casablanca (1944)

2 Silence of the Lambs (1992)

3 Schindler's List (1994)

4 Shak

6 Slumdog Millionaire (2009)

7 Chariots of Fire (1982)

8 The King's Speech (2011)

9 Godfather Part I (1972)

10 Godfather Part II (1975)

11 Danc

13 Lawrence of Arabia (1963)

14 Chicago (2003)

15 West Side Story (1962)

16 The Lord of the Rings (2004)

17 Gladiator (2001)

18

20 Forrest Gump (1995)

21 The Sound of Music (1966)

22 Titanic (1998)

23 Annie Hall (1978)

24 Rocky (1977)

26 The E

27 My Fair Lady (1965)

28 Braveheart (1996)

29 2012 Oscar's Winner

Amer

In celebration of this years Oscars, we've compiled a list of your favourite Academy Award Best Picture winners, as voted for by you.

Every night throughout the whole of February we're giving you the opportunity to watch these classics for one last time on the big screen, along with the chance to win big prizes that include an all inclusive weekend trip for two to Los Angeles.

Sunday

5

...Love (1999)   Oliver! (1968)

12

...olves (1991)   Gone with the Wind (1940)

19

...tient (1997)   Rain Man (1988)

26

...uty (2004)   Platoon (1987)

Oscar Winners Month
February Listings

Monday	Tuesday	Wednesday	Thursday
		Casablanca (1944)	Silence of the
Slumdog Millionaire (2009)	Chariots of Fire (1982)	The King's Speech (2010)	Godfather Part
Lawrence of Arabia (1963)	Chicago (2003)	West Side Story (1962)	The Lord of the
Forrest Gump (1995)	The Sound of Music (1966)	Titanic (1996)	Annie Hall (197
My Fair Lady (1966)	Braveheart (1996)	2012 Oscars Winner TBA	

Booking Information
Box Office: 0113 224 4601
Main Office: 0113 245 7740

Online
www.thecarriageworks.co.uk
info@thecarriageworks.co.uk

The Carriageworks
The Carriageworks
3 Millennium Square
Leeds LS2 3AD

Friday	Saturday	Sunday

(1992) Schindler's List (1994) Shakespeare in Love (1998) Oliver! (1968)

Godfather Part II (1975) Dances With Wolves (1991) Gone with the Wind (1940)

(2004) Gladiator (2000) The English Patient (1997) Rain Man (1989)

Rocky (1977) American Beauty (2004) Platoon (1987)

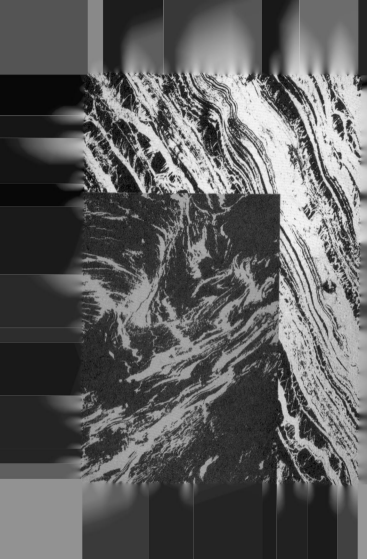

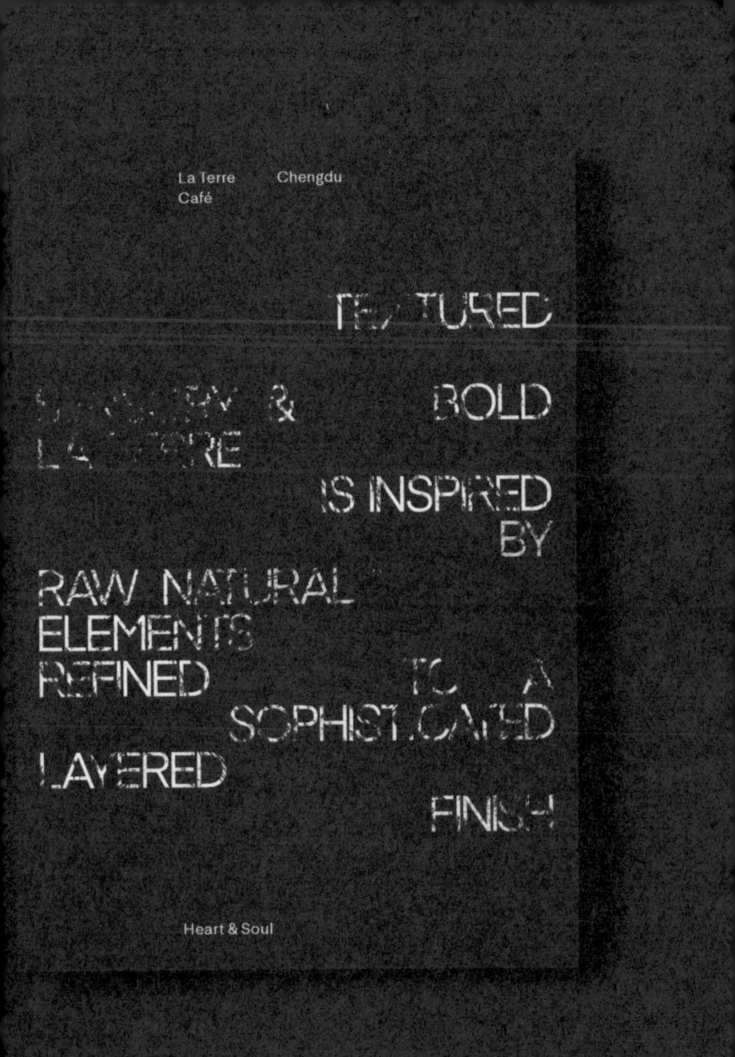

La Terre Café   Chengdu

TEXTURED

LUXURY &   BOLD
LA TERRE

IS INSPIRED
BY

RAW NATURAL
ELEMENTS
REFINED   TO   A
SOPHISTICATED
LAYERED

FINISH

Heart & Soul

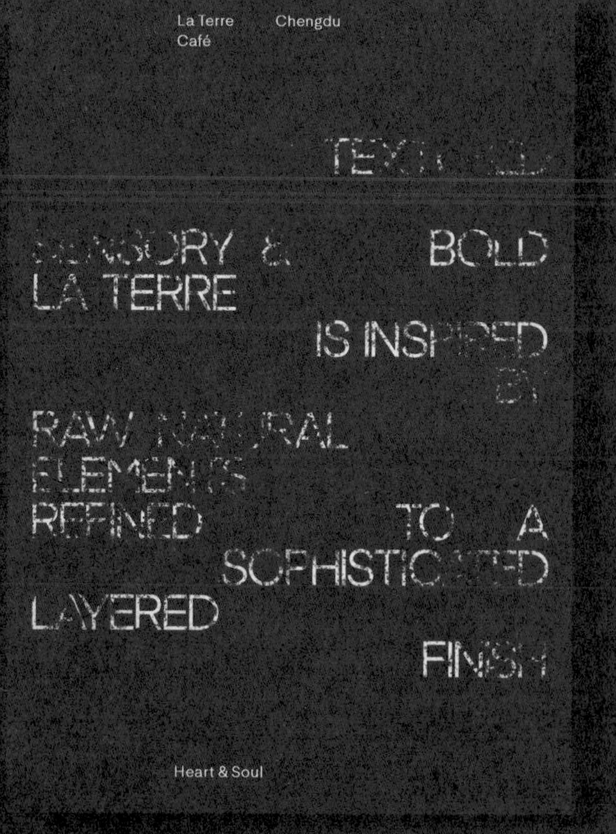

La Terre
Café

Chengdu

TEXTURED

SENSORY & BOLD
LA TERRE
IS INSPIRED
BY

RAW NATURAL
ELEMENTS
REFINED
TO A
SOPHISTICATED
LAYERED
FINISH

Heart & Soul

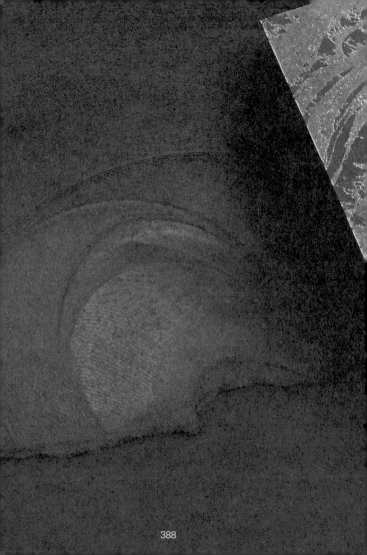

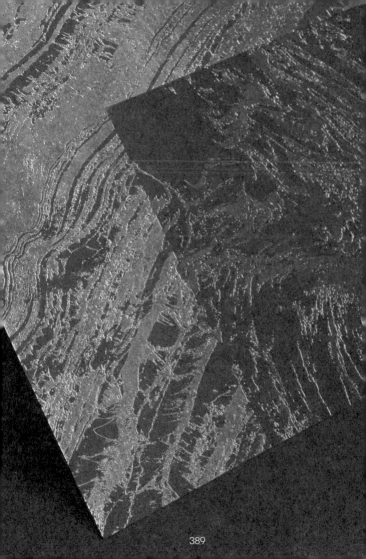

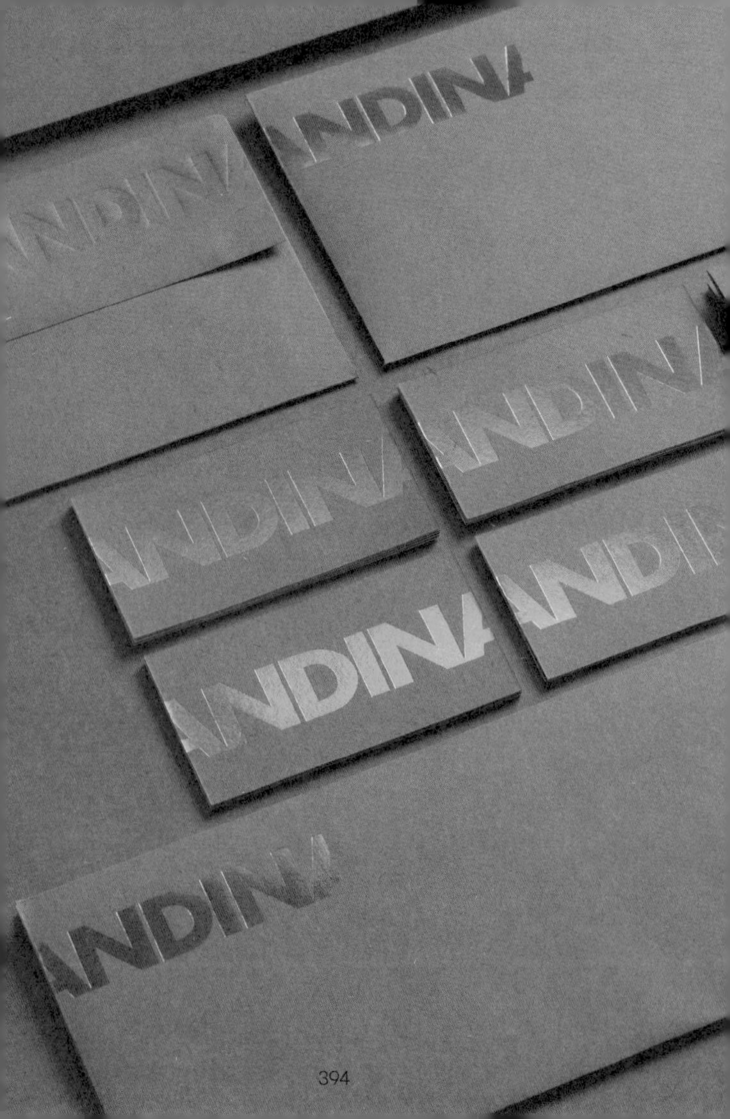

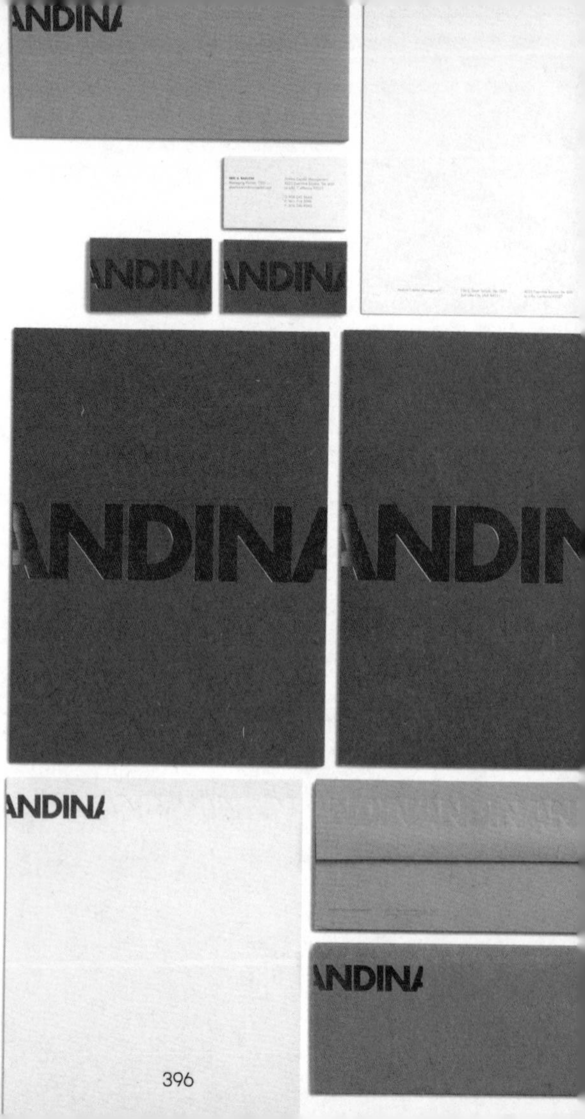

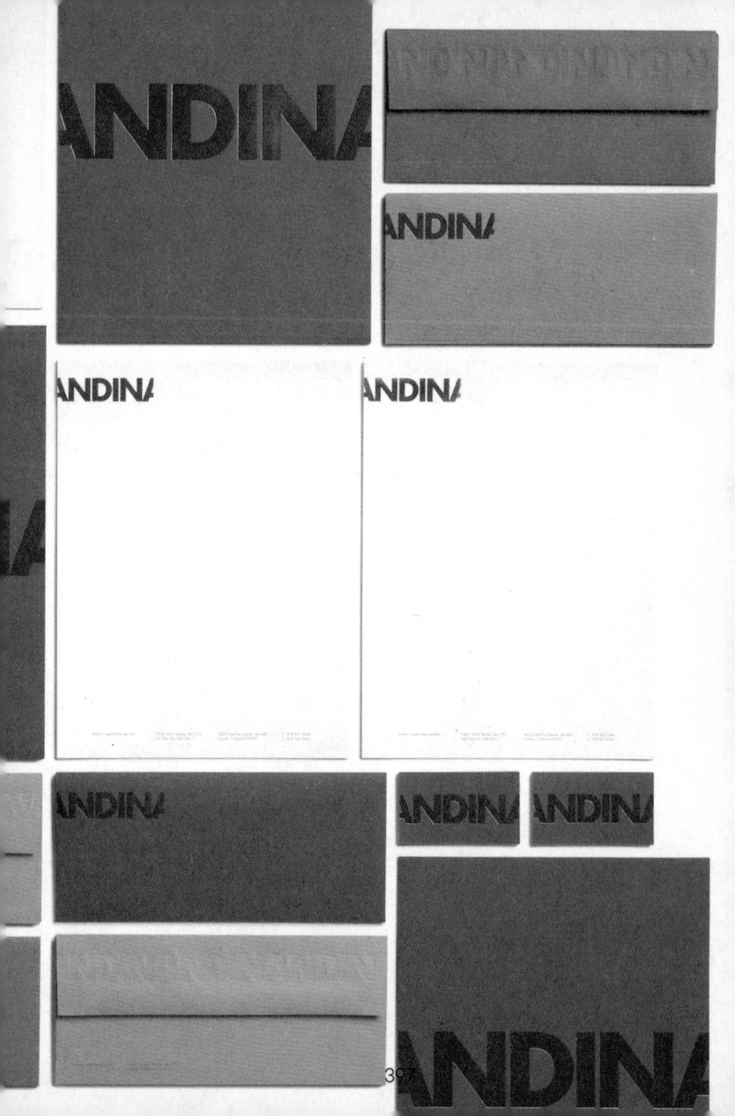

The New York Times

"All the News
That's Fit to Print"

The New York Times

Late Edition
New York: Today, sunny, a low afternoon clouds. High 77. Tonight, mostly clear, low 61. Tomorrow, sunshine then clouds. High 81. Yesterday, High 81, low 66. Weather map, Page C18.

VOL. CL ... No. 51,874   NEW YORK, WEDNESDAY, SEPTEMBER 12, 2001   75 CENTS

"All the News
That's Fit to Print"

The New York Times

Late Edition

VOL. CLXI ... No. 55,564

NEW YORK, THURSDAY, OCTOBER 20, 2011

$2.00

410

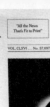

 Late Edition

The New York Times

"All the News That's Fit to Print"

VOL. CLXVI... No. 57,697

NEW YORK, TUESDAY, AUGUST 22, 2017

$2.50

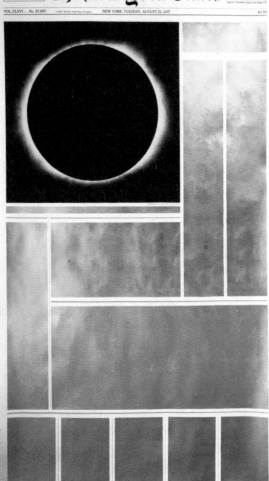

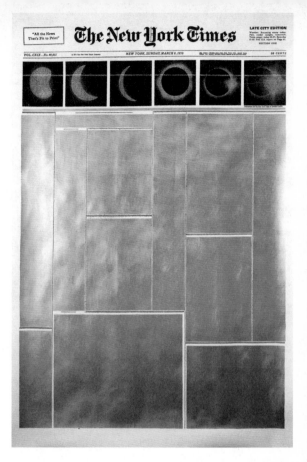

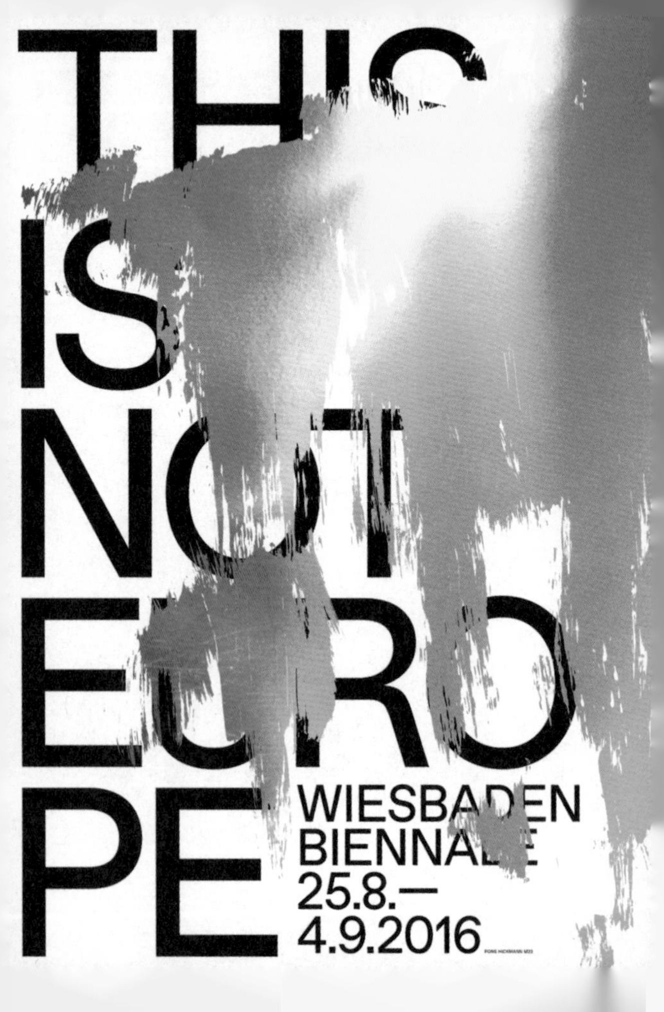

THIS IS NOT EUROPE

WIESBADEN
BIENNALE
25.8.—
4.9.2016

THIS
IS
NO
EURO
PE
WIESBA..
BIENNALE
25.8.—
4.9.2016

DAS ASYL DES
MÜDEN EU..
...HENON METOPES,

HESSISCHES
STAATSTHEATER
...

DIE BEWEGUNG:
DIE ARMEE DER LIEBE,
Dora Garcia & Ingo N...

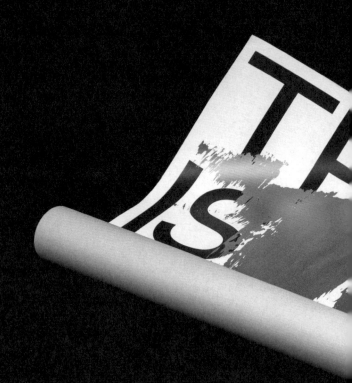

WIESBADEN
BIENNALE
25.8.
4.9.2016

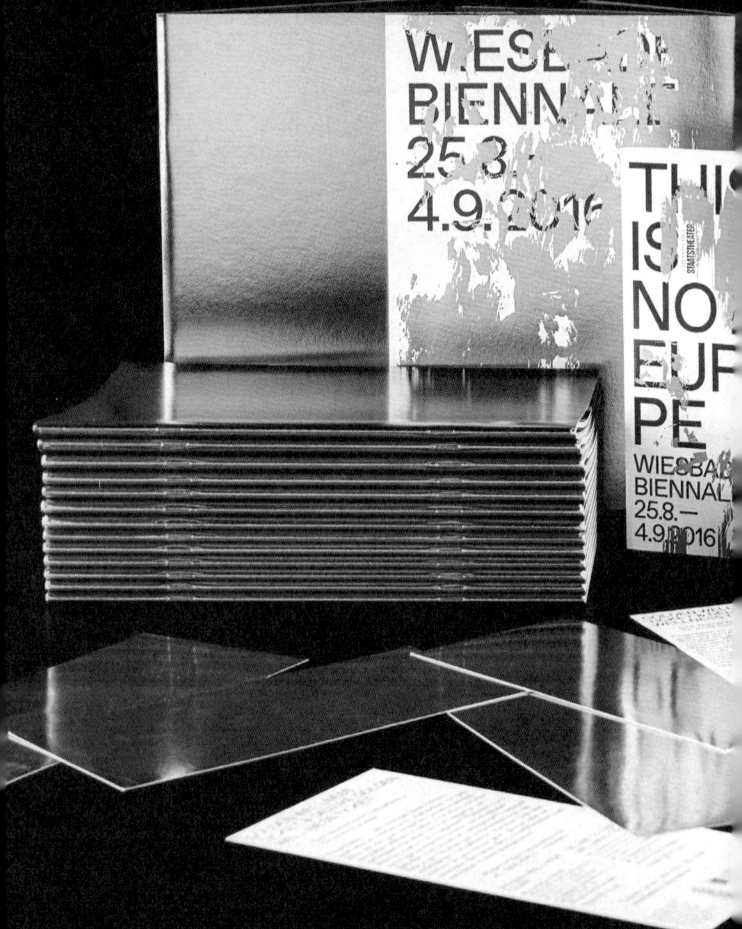
THIS
IS
NO
EU
PE
WIESBA
BIENNAL
25.8.—
4.9.2016
STAATSTHEATER

THIS
IS
NO
EURO
PE

WIESBADEN
BIENNALE
25.8.—
4.9.2016

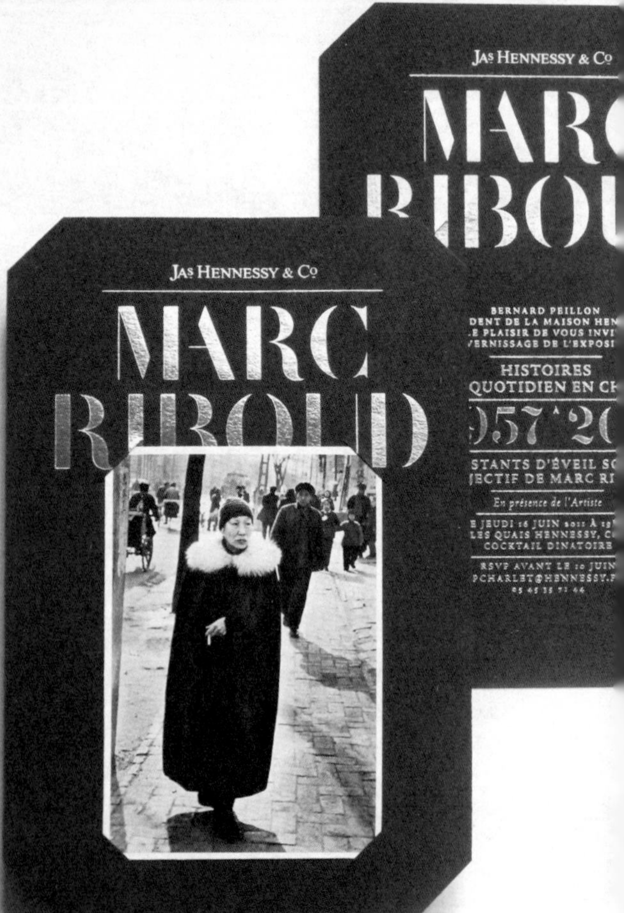

JAS HENNESSY & CO
MARC
RIBOUD
BERNARD PEILLON
HISTOIRES
En présence de l'Artiste
COCKTAIL DINATOIRE

" LES PAYS QUE J'AIME
SONT COMME DES AMIS,
J'AIME LES REVOIR, SAVOIR
CE QU'ILS DEVIENNENT,
COMMENT ILS CHANGENT.
AINSI JE RETOURNE
SOUVENT EN CHINE OÙ
TOUT BOUGE PLUS VITE
QU'AILLEURS. MÊME SI L'ŒIL
ATTENTIF PEUT VOIR SOUS
CETTE SURFACE AGITÉE
LE FIL DE LA CONTINUITÉ. "

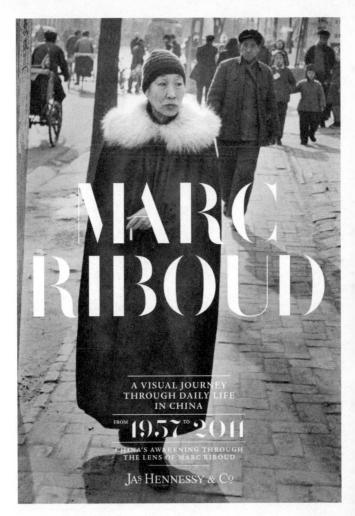

MARC RIBOUD

A VISUAL JOURNEY
THROUGH DAILY LIFE
IN CHINA

FROM 1957 TO 2011

CHINA'S AWAKENING THROUGH
THE LENS OF MARC RIBOUD

JAS HENNESSY & CO

LES
DES
CE Q
CHA
EN O
QU'S
PEU
LE F

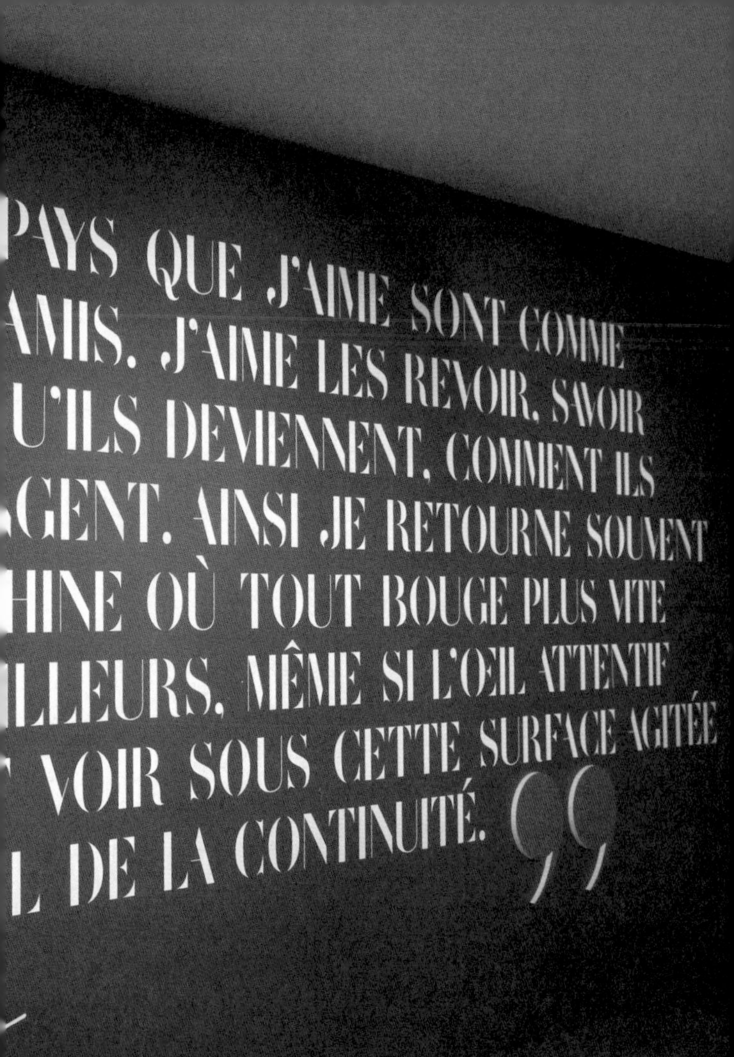

PAYS QUE J'AIME SONT COMME

AMIS. J'AIME LES REVOIR, SAVOIR

U'ILS DEVIENNENT, COMMENT ILS

GENT. AINSI JE RETOURNE SOUVENT

HINE OÙ TOUT BOUGE PLUS VITE

LLEURS, MÊME SI L'OEIL ATTENTIF

VOIR SOUS CETTE SURFACE AGITÉE

L DE LA CONTINUITÉ. 99

Nº 48 | 2012

JEOPARDY

MAGAZINE

White Owl

THE CIGARS HEREIN CONTAINED
HAVE MANUFACTURED BELOW A
WHOLESALE, EACH AND
MADE MORE THAN 6'S EACH
AND ARE SO TAX PAID.

Invincibles

JEOPARDY MAGAZINE | Nº 48 | 2012

EST 1974

MAISON
GERARD

NEW YORK

SLANTED

LIGHT
BOLD
LIGHT

Bold / Light

Slanted 16
Winter 2011
Typography &
Graphic Design
ISSN 1867-6510

Germany € 12
Switzerland CHF 25
UK £ 16
USA $ 26
Others € 16

SLANTED

Slanted 16 — Bold / Light
Slanted 16 — Bold / Light
Slanted 16 — Bold / Light
Slanted 16 — Bold / Light
Slanted 16 — Bold / Light
Slanted 16 — Bold / Light

Bold / Light

ISBN 1897-2810
Graphic Design
Typography
Winter 2011
Started in Portugal

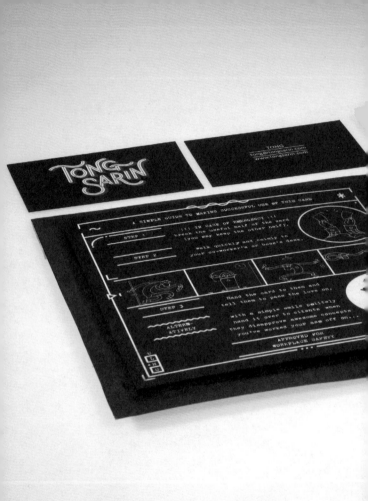

TONG
SARIN

TONG
tong@tongsarin.com
www.tongsarin.com

A SIMPLE GUIDE TO MAKING SUCCESSFUL USE OF THIS CARD

!!! IN CASE OF EMERGENCY !!!
break the useful half of the card
(you may keep the other half).

STEP 1

Walk quickly and calmly to
your co-worker's or boss's desk.

STEP 2

Hand the card to them and
tell them to pass the love on.

STEP 3

ALTERN-
ATIVELY

with a simple smile politely
hand it over to clients when
they disapprove awesome concepts
you've worked your ass off on...

APPROVED FOR
WORKPLACE SAFETY

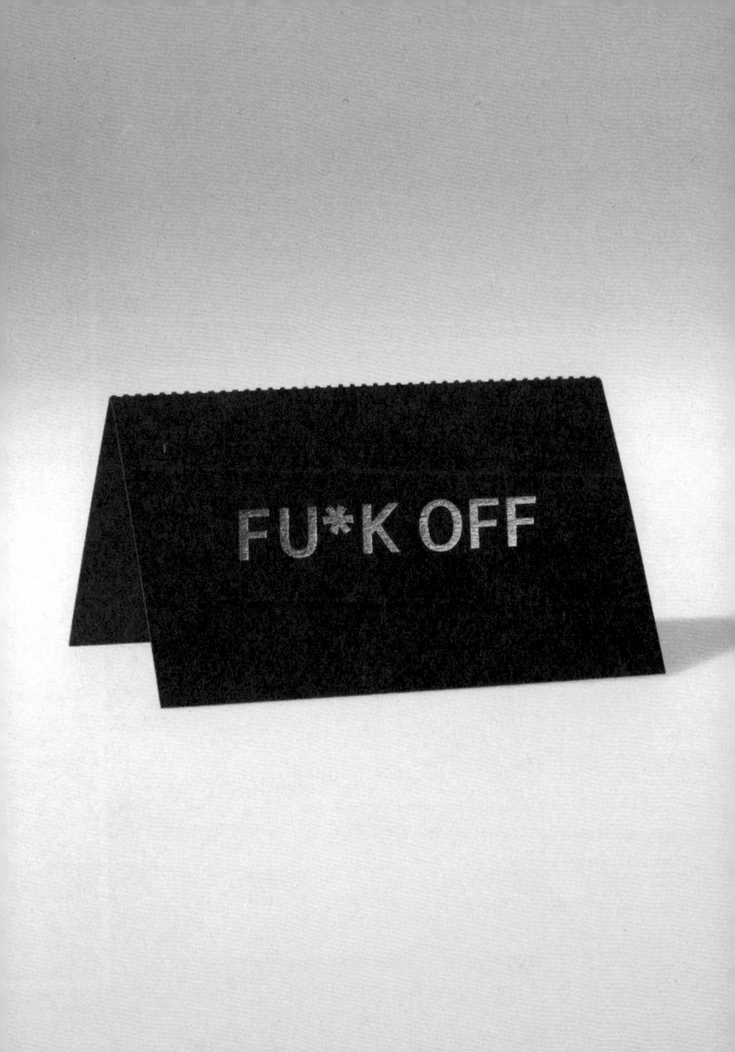
FU*K OFF

"Metallic shades mix worlds, artificial and material, together."

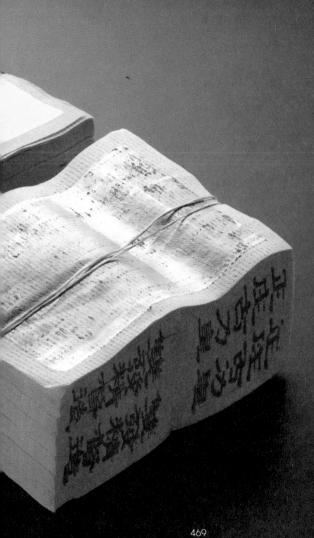

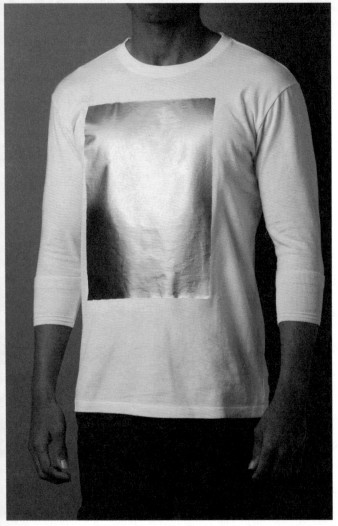

473

鏡之書

THE BOOK OF MIRRORS

尤金・切洛維奇——著

李建興——譯

E.O. Chirovici

鏡之書

THE
BOOK
OF
MIRRORS

E.O. Chirovici

尤金·切洛維
李建興

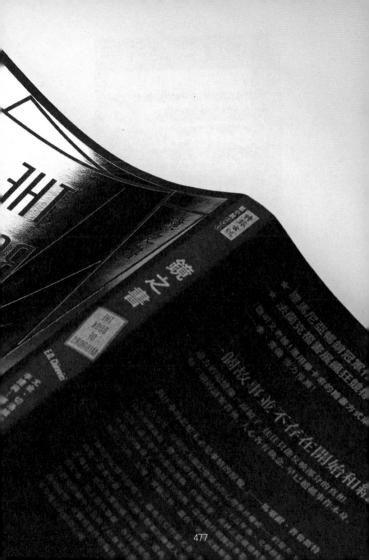

Ryan McGinness

Calendar
To-Do List
Pad

2013
365 Drawings

Published by Gingko Press
gingkopress.com

**Every day
a different drawing.
Every day
things to do.**

483

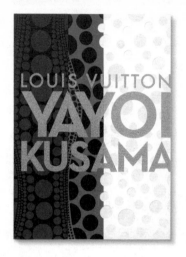

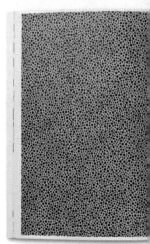

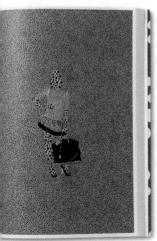

La Casa Encendi

Edward Gordon Craig.
El espacio como espectáculo

Del 19 de noviembre de
al 17 de enero de 2010

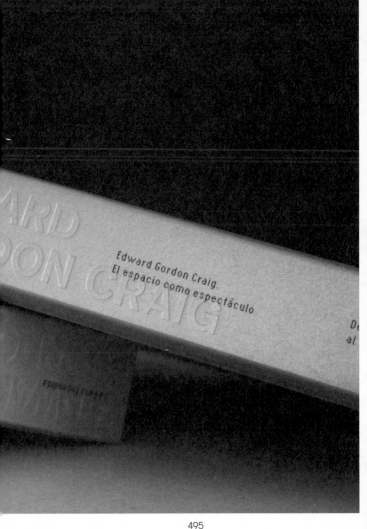

Edward Gordon Craig.
El espacio como espectáculo

Kungl.
Konsthögskolans
Examensutställning
Magister 2010

The Royal
Institute of Art
Degree Show 2010

Knock Knock!
Who's there?
Sade!
Sade who?
Sade Coy!

505

506

ANAYI

essence of
ANAYI

allureville

**AUTUMN & WINTER 2012-2013
COLLECTION PRESENTATION**

Date & Time
May 17th (Thu) -18th (Fri) 11:00~18:00

Place
THE RITZ-CARLTON, TOKYO 1F

ANAYI: The Cypress Room
essence of ANAYI: The Maple Room
allureville: The Garden Room

THE MONDAY ROOM

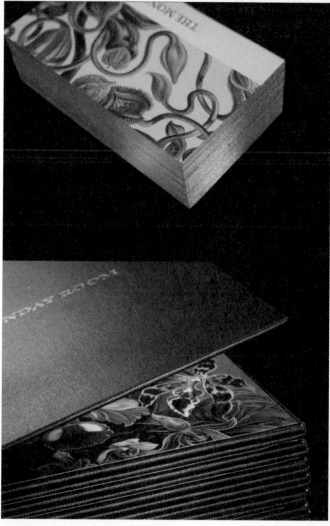

groovewear / www.groovewear.it

Groovewear is rhythm, passion, music and art. The project created with an idea in mind: to improve the colors and shapes of street art on paper or fabric.

...is not any wrapping, but in a handmade box containing one of the artist's screen prints, numbered and printed by craftsmen. Not just a simple garment, but a t-shirt personalized with the utmost care of its fabric, workmanship and design. Two unique objects combining innovation, craftsmanship and high quality typical of Made in Italy.

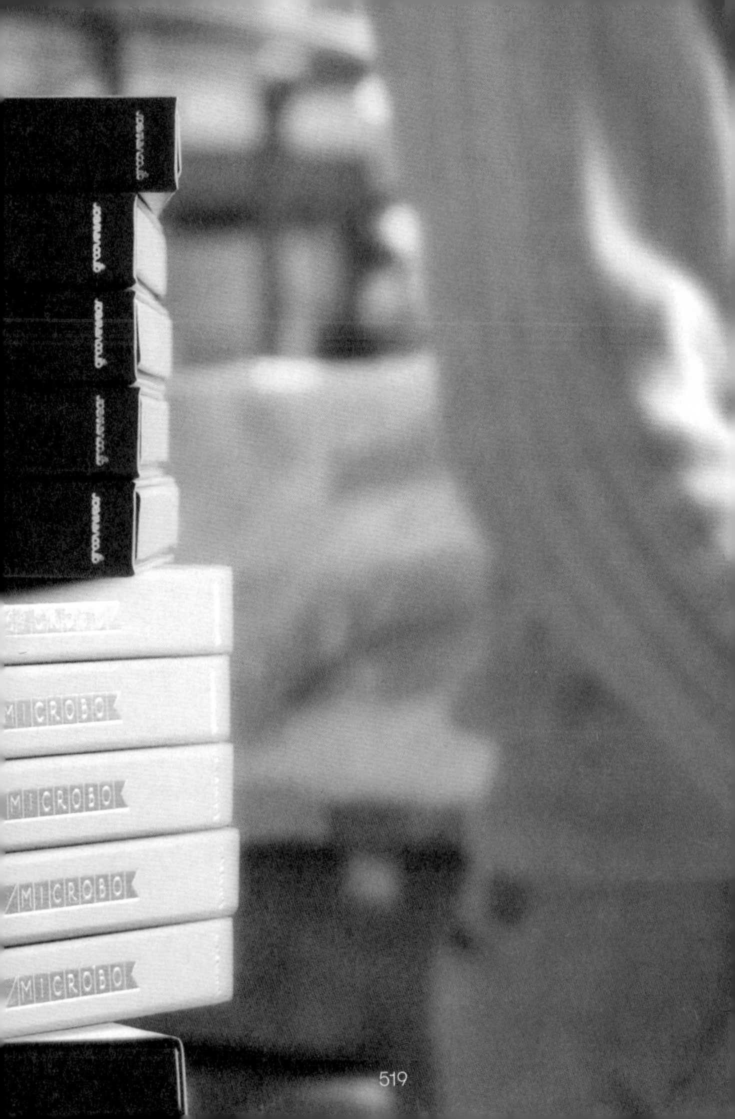
MICROBO
MICROBO
MICROBO
MICROBO

Art
Objects of Virtu
Contemporary
Jewellery

Belmacz • 45 Davies Street • Lon
TEL: +44 (0)20 7629 7863 • FAX:
EMAIL: gallery@belmacz.com • www.

be macz

be macz

525

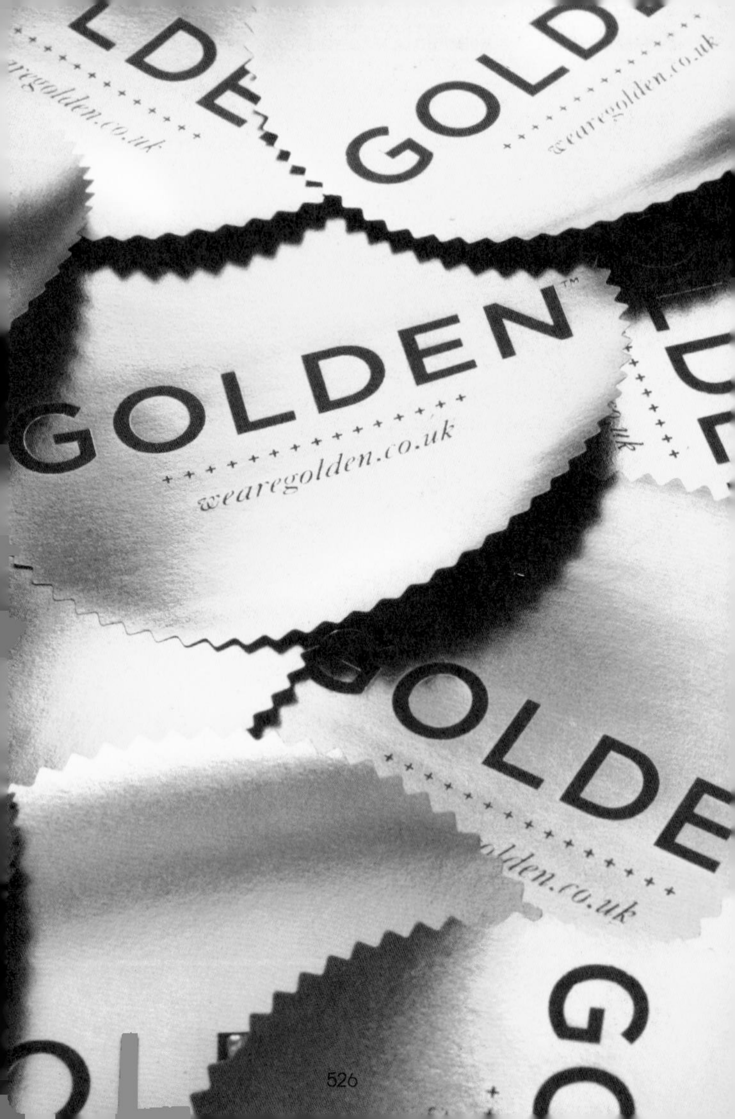
GOLDEN™
wearegolden.co.uk

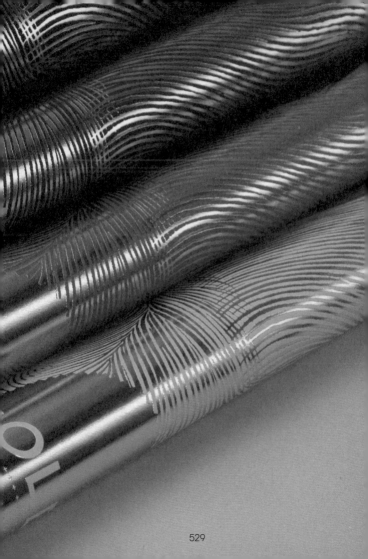

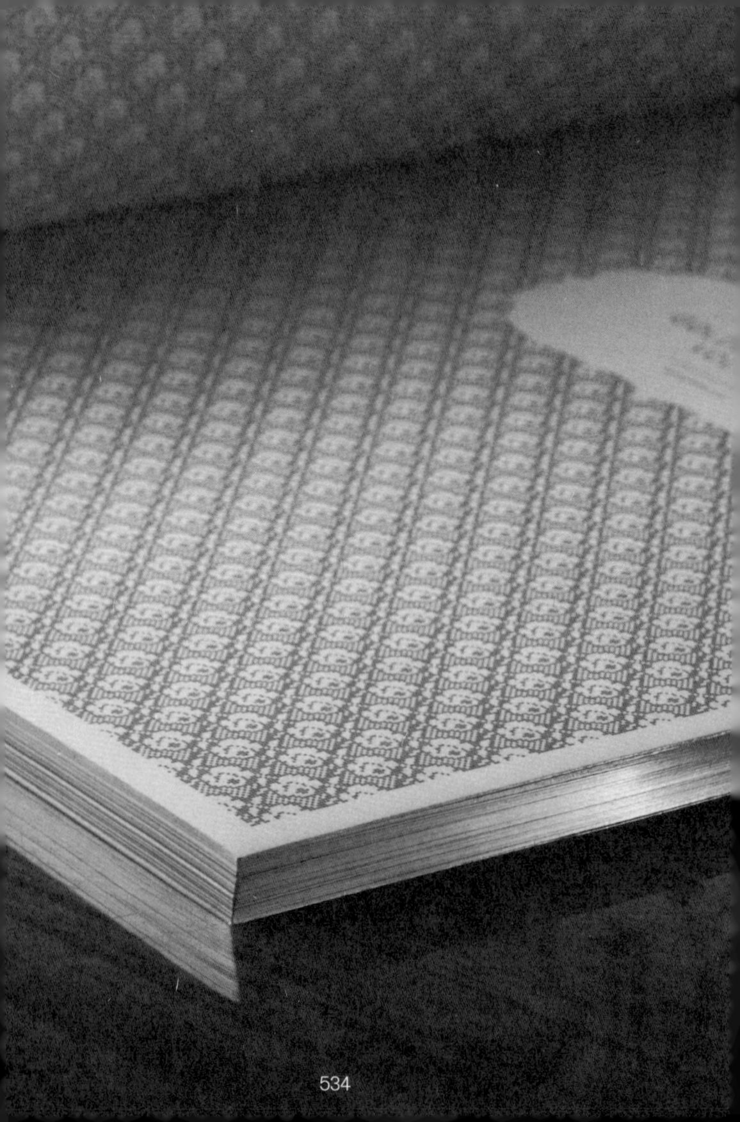

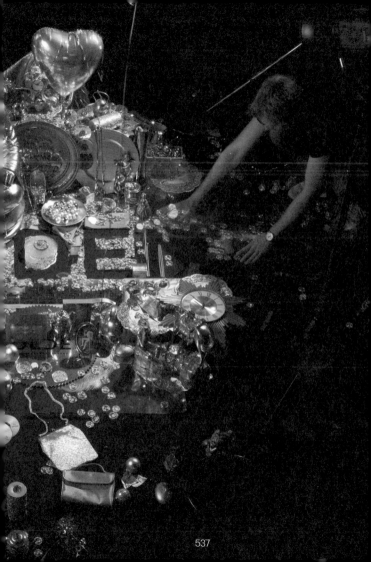

"Gold is an important symbolic element for the Mayan culture among many other civilisations. Gold marks the year of the publication, as well as the creative talents featured inside."

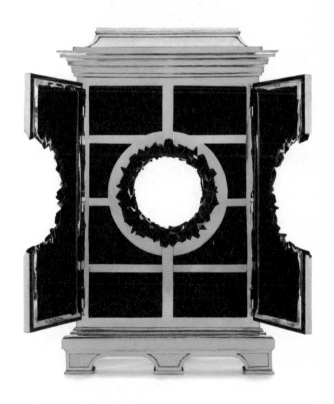

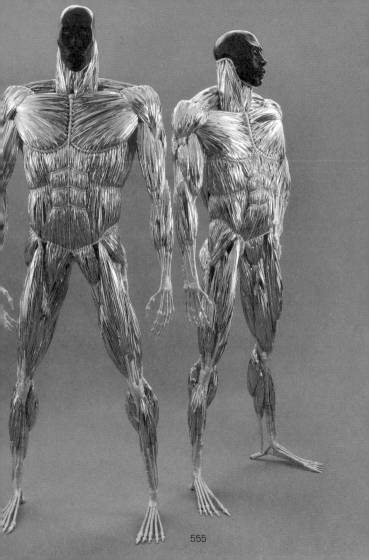

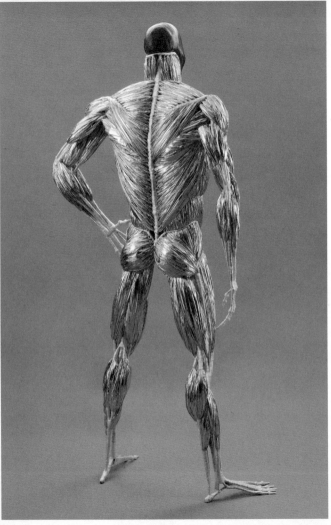

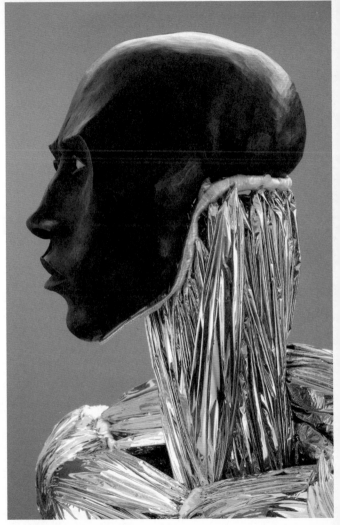

Systems, 25 November — 31 December, 2013
Walter Knoll London showroom, 42 Charterhouse Square EC1M 6EA
An exhibition curated by das programm. Produced in association with BRAUN
Poster by Neubau. Designed in Germany.

564

6% ABV · 33 CENTILITER
Mosaic, Citra, Wheat, Oats, Barley
Innehåller kornmalt. Starköl.

THAT GENUINE CAN BEER FLAVOUR! · PANGPANG CAN RELEASE ·
THAT GENUINE CAN BEER FLAVOUR! · PANGPANG CAN RELEASE ·
PANGPANG CAN RELEASE · THAT GENUINE CAN BEER
BEER FLAVOUR! · THAT GENUINE CAN RELEASE ·

PANGPANG CAN RELEASE · THAT GENUINE CAN BEER FLAVOUR! ·
PANGPANG CAN RELEASE · THAT GENUINE CAN BEER FLAVOUR! ·
PANGPANG CAN RELEASE · THAT GENUINE CAN BEER FLAVOUR! ·

5 HANOVER SQUARE

LONDON W1

On behalf of Mitsui Fudosan and Stanhope Plc,
you are cordially invited to a cocktail party to celebrate
the launch of 5 Hanover Square W1

ADDRESS:
5 HANOVER SQUARE W1

DATE:
WEDNESDAY MARCH 28TH

TIME:
FROM 5.30PM

PLEASE RSVP TO:
Charlotte Hopton-Scott
Email: charlotte.hopton-scott@stanhopeplc.com
Telephone: 020 7170 1647

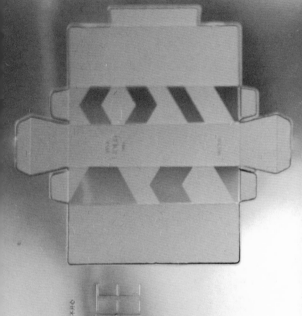

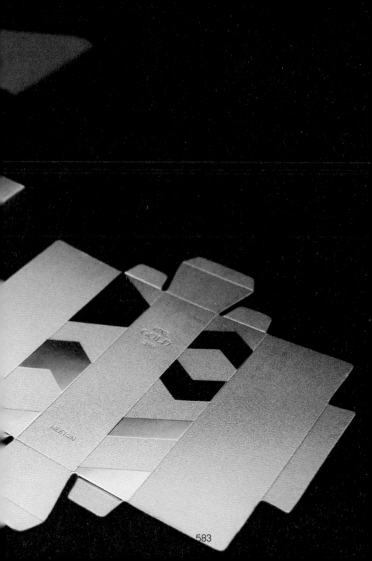

NEW AGE

MEETON
有旺

MEETON

旺

ER 57
E R E V A N

SHAMPOO

1

"I long,
as does every
human being, to be
at home wherever
I find myself."

South Ulster Housing Association
2008 Annual Report

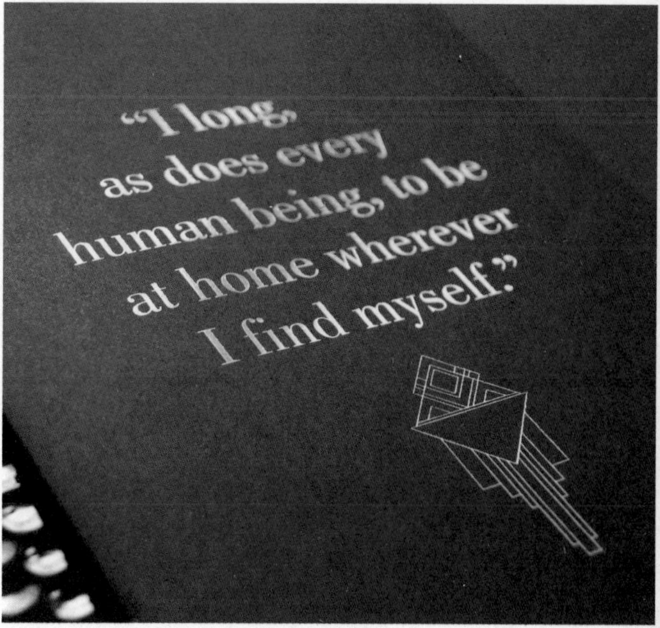

"I long,
as does every
human being, to be
at home wherever
I find myself."

02.16.09

3.4

IDeeeN

14:10

THE FRAGMENT ASSEMBLY. shatter
B1-16 SHINJUKU SHIBUYA KU TOKYO JP
OPEN WEEKDAY 12:00–22:00 SATURDAY 9AM–9AM
BY APPOINTMENT

6|30

Grand
Opening 11A.M.

THE FRAGMENT ASSEMBLY, shatter
B72/4-1 JINGUMAE SHIBUYA-KU, TOKYO
OPEN WEEKDAY / SATURDAY & SUNDAY / TUESDAY CLOSED

7|02

Reception
Party 18P.M.

sha

tter

603

Thursday December 13th 2007 Cologne Store Opening

Freakout till you blackout

Lee Store Opening Party
Donnerstag,
13. Dezember 2007
Ab 19.30 Uhr
Fingerfood, Drinks
mit DJ Cram

Lee Store Köln
Friesenwall 3
50672 Köln

Freakout Live Concert
Ab 22.00 Uhr
mit Kilians und
Men'box
"Ferris Mc. Marc Deal"

Gästeliste
Hans-Böckler-Platz 2
50672 Köln

Shuttle Service
Ab 22.00 Uhr

Shop till you Drop Key
25% Bonus in allen
deutschen Lee Stores.
Auf alles, nur für
Dich und für immer.

"Metallic colours have a very particular brightness. We intend to create a new atmosphere by unifying shapes and forms."

INDEX

010	**Polyhedra Notebook** Present & Correct
011	**Shapes Postcard** Present & Correct
012–019	**Best Awards Identity** Alt Group Client: Designers Institute of New Zealand Photo: Toaki Okano
020–025	**Sugar Paper Products** Sugar Paper Los Angeles Calligraphy: (Bubbly Cheers) Lisa Holtzman Illustration: (Ampersand) Joanna Reynolds Photo: Diana Reith
026–029	**Verena Michelitsch Business Cards** Verena Michelitsch Printing: THE IF
030–033	**Sourcing Studio Identity** Artiva Design Client: Sourcing Studio
034–037	**Lo Siento by Mucho** Mucho, Pablo Juncadella Client: Lo Siento

038–043 **The Collection**
Mind Design

Client: The Collection
Interior design: Design Research Studio

044–047 **Marou Chocolate**
Rice Creative

Client: Marou Faiseurs De Chocolat
Photo: Arnaud De Harven

048–051 **Marou Wallpaper* Handmade**
Rice Creative

Client: Marou Faiseurs De Chocolat,
Wallpaper* Magazine
Photo: Arnaud De Harven

052–059 **Cokoa**
Giada Tamborrino

061–063 **Tricolette Identity**
KentLyons

Client: Tricolette

064–067 **Department Of Architecture
Course Catalogue**
G Design Studio

Client: University of Patras, Department of Architecture

068–071   **Nevertheless Magazine #02**
atelier olschinsky

072–075   **Christmas in July**
Foundry

Client: Liberty

076–079   **Notebook Project**
Deutsche & Japaner

Client: Imprimerie du Marais

080–087   **GF Smith Master Selector**
SEA

Client: GF Smith

088–095   **Maison Dandoy ID**
Base Design (Brussels)

Client: Maison Dandoy

096–099   **The Golden Set**
Furze Chan

100–105   **The Reopening of Pagoda at
Chinzan-so Garden**
Nippon Design Center, Inc.

Client: Fujita Kanko
Public relations: Takuro Nishino, Fujita Kanko
Photo: Shun Takano

107–111	**Upgrade**
	Tomas Kral
	Photo: Michel Bonvin

112–115	**The Letters Poster**
	55 Hi's
	Typography: 55 Hi's, Richard Perez (aka Skinny Ships)

116–117	**Nike 255 Custom Lab Collateral**
	Darrin Crescenzi
	Client: Nike Sportswear
	Printing: Premier Press (Portland, USA)

118–121	**Gabriel Saunders Identity**
	Takt Studio
	Client: Gabriel Saunders

122–125	**Xstrata Coal Singapore Packaging**
	End of Work
	Client: Xstrata Coal Singapore

126–129	**In Gold We Trust**
	Blank
	Client: Creneau int

130–133   **IN&OUT**
Guang Yu

134–141   **F. Scott Fitzgerald**
Coralie Bickford-Smith

142–153   **The Kaleidoscopic Eye**
ujidesign

Client: Mori Art Museum,
Thyssen-Bornemisza Art Contemporary
Photo: (Environment) Takumi Ota,
(Collateral) Masaya Onozato

154–155   **Berliner Zimmer, Sarajevo**
Designers United

Client: Goethe Institute Thessaloniki

156–159   **Warhol sobre Warhol**
Base Design (Madrid)

Client: La Casa Encendida

160–165   **Y-3 Store Opening Invite & Lookbook**
Greige.

Client: Häberlein und Mauerer AG (Berlin)
Photo: Mario Sorrenti (Campaign), Martin Müller
(Lookbook)

166–177 **2017 Brand New Conference Identity**
UnderConsideration LLC

178–185 **Gild**
Mucho

Client: Gild

186–189 **G8**
mintdesigns

Client: Kulturprojekte Berlin GmbH

190–197 **Placebo Pharmacy**
Luminous Design Group

199–205 **First Floor**
Luminous Design Group

206–209 **HKIA 2010**
c plus c workshop

210–217 **Neat Confections**
Anagrama Studio

Client: Neat Confections
Photo: Caroga Foto / carogafoto.com

218–221	**Roma Alphabet Book** A3.Format Group
	Illustration: Milica Pantelić, Željko Lončar, Ivan Petruševski, Nenad Trifunović, Nebojša Cvetković, Jurij Lozić, Iva Spasojević, Primož Zorko, Filip Pomykalo, Marijana Zarić
222–223	**Institut Parfumeur Flores** Bunch
	Client: Institut Parfumeur Flores
224–235	**The Golden Age 999.9 Notebook Gift Box** MANMANTEAM Design Office Inc.
	Client: TEUAN Photo: Dawei Yang
236–239	**New Zealand Music** Alt Group
	Client: New Zealand Trade and Entreprise Photo: Toaki Okano
241–243	**Modezonen Invite & Catalogue** Homework / Jack Dahl
	Client: Modezonen
244–247	**Grantpirrie – Hong Kong Art Fair 2010** Collider
	Client: Grantpirrie

248–253 **La Vittoria Branding**
lg2

Client: La Vittoria (Nathalie LeProhon, Johanne Demers)
Creative direction: Claude Auchu
Art direction/design: Anne-Marie Clermont,
Maude Lescarbeau, Éric Bouchard
Copywriting: Pierre Lussier
Web design: Éric Bouchard

255–267 **LUNAR SAMPLE RETURN Edition**
ANICORN WATCHES

268–269 **Look At Me Now**
Peter Tarka Design

270–271 **Typography**
Peter Tarka Design

272–279 **Insert RIO**
Plenty

Client: Insert RIO

280–283 **BAPE® ARCHIVES by NIGO®**
groovisions

Client: honeyee.com Inc.

284–291 **Argyll Brand Identity**
Nelson Associates

292–295   **Liberty Renaissance VIP Invite**
Foundry

296–301   **Komplizen der Spielregeln 2011**
Deutsche & Japaner

Client: Komplizen der Spielregeln

302–303   **FOR HUMAN (JAPAN)**
KOTENHITS

Client: HITSFAMILY

304–307   **Deutsche & Japaner Corporate**
Deutsche & Japaner

308–311   **B1234**
Lo Siento

Client: BAD | Built by Associative Data

312–315   **Mathias Tanguy Visual Identity**
DMWORKROOM

Client: Mathias Tanguy

316–321   **Catalina Fernandez Branding**
Anagrama Studio

Client: Catalina Fernandez

| 322–323 | **MABE**
Studio Band |
| | Client: MABE Hair |

| 325 | **London MMXII**
BERG |
| | Author: Angela Law
Client: kubrick (Hong Kong) |

| 326–327 | **LAF invitation**
Edgar Bąk |
| | Client: Atom Cinema |

| 328–341 | **HKDA Global Design Awards 2011**
c plus c workshop |
| | Client: Hong Kong Designer Association (HKDA) |

| 342–347 | **Penny Royal Films**
Alphabetical |
| | Client: Penny Royal Films
Printing: Identity |

| 348–349 | **London 2012 Olympic Games Posters**
Chris Clarke |
| | Printing: Luma Studio (London) |

350–365   **Singular**
Futura

Photo: Rodrigo Chapa

366–369   **Golden Mermaid.**
Paco Peregrin

Client: VISION Magazine (China)
Styling: Mario Ville (Kattaca)
Makeup: Lewis Amarante
Models: Bel Sánchez (UNO Models)

371–373   **Tiger Beer — Business Card**
Jon Chapman-Smith / Fuman

Printing: Plasmark LTD.

374–379   **The Carriageworks**
John Barton

Client: The Carriageworks

380–393   **La Terre**
Pop & Pac Studio

Photo: Foliolio

394–397   **Andina Identity**
Hint Creative

Client: Andina Captial Management
Photo: Derek Israelsen

398–405 **Nike Retail Hospitality**
Darrin Crescenzi

Client: Nike, Inc.
Creative direction: Andy Walker
Printing: Premier Press (Portland, USA)

406–413 **Gold New York Times**
Panos Tsagaris

PP. 406–407: Nigredo
Courtesy of the artist and Kalfayan Galleries, Athens-
Thessaloniki. Original newspaper photos by Pantelis
Saitas/European PressPhoto Agency (P.406) and Zakaria
Abdelkafi/Agence France-Presse - Getty Images (P.407).

P. 408: September 12 2001
Courtesy of the artist and Kalfayan Galleries, Athens-
Thessaloniki. Original newspaper photo by Steve Ludlum.

P. 409: June 30 2011
Courtesy of the artist and Kalfayan Galleries, Athens-
Thessaloniki. Original newspaper photo by John
Kolesidis/Reuters.

P. 410: October 20 2011
Courtesy of the artist and Kalfayan Galleries, Athens-
Thessaloniki. Original newspaper photo by Yannis
Behrakis/Reuters.

P. 411: February 13 2012
Courtesy of the artist and Kalfayan Galleries, Athens-
Thessaloniki. Original newspaper photo by Angelos
Tzortzinis/Agence France-Presse - Getty Images.

P. 412: August 22 2017
Courtesy of the artist and Kalfayan Galleries, Athens-
Thessaloniki. Original newspaper photo by Timothy D.
Easley/Associated Press.

P. 413: March 8 1970
Courtesy of the artist and Kalfayan Galleries, Athens-
Thessaloniki. Original newspaper photo by Ernest Sisto/
New York Times.

414–421	This Is Not Europe Fons Hickmann m23
422–427	MARC RIBOUD Exhibition Leslie David Client: Hennessy
428–433	À Volta do Barroco Sara Westermann, Casa da Música Client: Casa da Música
434–441	Jeopardy No.48 Catherine Renee Dimalla Client: Jeopardy Magazine Art direction/editing: Erik Fenner
442–445	Maison Gerard Identity & Collateral Mother New York Client: Maison Gerard
446–449	Slanted Magazine #16 — Bold / Light Slanted Magazine & Weblog
450–455	Exclusive Bike Services KONG STUDIO Client: EXCLUSIVE BIKE SERVICES

456–457   **Plenty's Business Card**
           Plenty

458–461   **Tong Sarin Promotional Package**
           Tong Sarin

           Illustration: Christopher Cooper
           Design: (Logo) Julian Yeo

462–463   **Hours — 2012 Calendar**
           Mash Creative

465–467   **GOLDENHEN Business Cards**
           GOLDENHEN

           Photo: James Newman

468–473   **Hellbound**
           &Larry

474–477   **The Book of Mirrors**
           Wei-Che Kao

           Client: China Times Publishing Co.

478–479   **To-Do-List Calendar 2013**
           Ryan McGinness

480–487   **Louis Vuitton — Yayoi Kusama Fine Book**
WORK

Client: Louis Vuitton Japan
Photo: WORK, Ivan Joshua Loh
Special credits: alsoDominie (Singapore),
ASHU Nakanishiya Co., Ltd.

488–491   **Jennifer Fisher Brand Book**
MyOrb

Client: Jennifer Fisher (JF)
Photo: Aaron Dyer

492–495   **El Espacio Como Espectáculo**
Base Design (Madrid)

Client: La Casa Encendida

496–499   **Royal Institute of Art Degree Show Catalogue**
Ritator

Client: Royal Institute of Art
Photo: Matti Östling

500–503   **Fiano di Avellino DOCG**
Basile Advertising

Client: Terre di Lapio

504–505   **Canon.**
Yogi Proctor

506–507	**Andrés Sardà X'mas Card** Mucho Client: Andrés Sardà
508–509	**ANAYI 2012 AW Collection Invitation** Nendesign inc. Client: FAR EAST COMPANY INC.
510–511	**Artisme 2012** Murmure Client: Artisme
512–515	**The Monday Room Identity** Strategy Design & Advertising Client: The Monday Room
516–519	**groovewear Artist Box** La Tigre Client: groovewear
520–523	**Belmacz Identity** Mind Design Client: Belmacz
524–531	**Golden Stationery** Golden

532–535	**Golden Moments II** Golden	
536–543	**Together We Are Golden.** Golden Photo: Andy Snaith	
545	**Sova Magazine 3 – Golden** Sova Magazine	
546–553	**Robber Baron** Studio Job Photo: Robert Kot	
554–557	**THE FIGHTING SOLAR BROS** Max Boufathal Client: The City of Saint-Quentin, France Photo: Claire Soubrier	
558–559	**The Batucada Collection** Jahara Studio	
560–563	**Profiles Project** Idan Friedman Photo: Dan Lev Studio	

564–567   **Braun Systems 2013 Ltd Poster Edition**
Neubau

Client: dasprogramm, Dr. Peter Kapos UK

568–575   **PangPang Can Release**
Jens Nilsson

Client: PangPang Brewery

576–577   **5 Handover Square Identity**
Winkreative

Client: Stanhope PLC/Mitsui Fudosan

578–579   **Aronia Juice Packaging**
Work in Progress

Client: Aronia Produkter BA

580–587   **Luck Package Design**
MEETON (Xiamen) Culture Communication Co.,
Ltd.

588–593   **Messier 53**
Backbone Branding

Client: Messier 53 Hotel Yerevan
Architect: Hayk Voskanyan

594–595   **SUHA Annual Report**
WILLOW

Client: South Ulster Housing Association (SUHA)

596–597   **IDEEËN AW 2009 Invitation**
STUDIO NEWWORK

598–601   **shatter**
Sitoh inc.

602–605   **Lee Store Opening**
Lloyd and Associates

Client: Lee Jeans

606–611   **Art Inflatable & Ephemeral**
Penique Productions

Special credits: Sala Dogana Hands-On Transformation

612–615   **Pålsjö Housing Project**
Wilhelmson Arkitekter

Client: HSB Nordvästra Skåne (Helsingborg, Sweden)

BIOGRAPHY

&Larry

andlarry.com

Founded in 2005, &Larry is a design company based in Singapore whose practice is deeply rooted in creating empathic connections between people. It believes that design innovation should always serve human interest — holding a high regard for the intuitive use of data, research, and technology in support of creativity instead of being limited by it.

PP. 468-473

55 Hi's

www.55his.com

A simple means of spreading inspiring quotes and quirky ideas, 55 Hi's (Fifty-Five Hi's) is a destination for graphic goodness, tasteful typography, and artful alliteration since its inception in 2010. Founded by Ross Moody, its clever and unique paper products are currently stocked in selected stores all around the world.

PP. 112-115

A3.Format Group

facebook.com/A3.Format

A3.Format is a self-publishing collective that was initiated in 2005 by Filip Bojović in Novi Sad with the help of Vladimir Manovski. A Yugoslav-born graphic designer, Filip is an avid analogue photographer who graduated in new visual media studies from the Academy of Arts in Novi Sad.

PP. 218-221

Alphabetical

alphabeticalstudio.com

Alphabetical is an award-winning creative graphics studio based in London. Founded in 2010 by Bob Young and Tommy Taylor, it focuses on creative thinking across a range of disciplines to produce designs with character and relevance on a variety of mediums.

PP. 342-347

Alt Group

altgroup.net

Based in Auckland, Alt Group is a multidisciplinary award-winning design studio founded in 2000 by Ben Corban and Dean Poole. Its core team consists of people from diversified backgrounds and experiences in design, business, brand strategy, communication design, interactive design, and new product development.

PP. 012-019, 236-239

Anagrama Studio

www.anagrama.com

With a focus on brand development and positioning, Anagrama Studio's services span the entire branding spectrum from strategic consulting to logotype and peripheral design. From its offices in Monterrey, Mexico City, Tokyo, and the US, it also creates objects, spaces, and multimedia experiences.

PP. 210-217, 316-321

ANICORN WATCHES
www.anicorn-watches.com

Anicorn Watches, a Hong Kong-based independent watch-maker and design studio, was founded in 2014 by Joe Kwan and Chris Chan to combine design, type, and mechanism through simplicity and contemporary style. Its products have been featured in design and lifestyle publications worldwide.

PP. 255-267

atelier olschinsky
www.olschinsky.at

Based in Vienna, atelier olschinsky was founded by Peter Olschinsky and Verena Weiss in 2002. The creative studio specialises in graphic design, illustration, photography, and art direction for clients, in addition to embarking on independent projects to develop and refine its craft.

PP. 068-071

Backbone Branding
backbonebranding.com

Backbone Branding is an independent branding studio in Armenia and a creative business partner to clients who are ready for extraordinary solutions. The team digs deep into a brand's essence and values – moving beyond design for design's sake to offer consumers solutions that are relevant and incredibly engaging.

PP. 588-593

Bąk, Edgar
www.edgarbak.info

Edgar Bąk is a Polish visual communication designer who avoids big gestures. By orienting himself to the tools at hand and their specificity, he focuses on the visual grammar and project brief – working towards the final outcome as if solving a mathematical equation. His eponymous studio focuses primarily on visual identity design.

PP. 326-327, 464

Barton, John
behance.net/johnbarton

A graduate of Leeds Metropolitan University, John Barton is a British graphic designer who is now freelancing for numerous well-established UK-based studios. Specialising in graphic design, branding, and typography, he enjoys screen-printing – taking up both commissioned work and independent projects.

PP. 374-379

Base Design
www.basedesign.com

Base is an international network of studios led by creatives in Brussels, New York, Geneva, and Melbourne. It works with clients on 360° branding solutions that encompass the traditional, physical, and digital worlds — building iconic brands through purpose, values, and vision.

PP. 088-095, 156-159, 492-495

Basile Advertising

www.andreabasile.it

Based in Italy, Basile Advertising is a dynamic agency that is committed to providing high-quality visual communication solutions that respond to the tastes and personalities of each client. Through branding and design, it creates a lasting presence for clients on the market through creative integrity.

PP. 500-503

BERG

BERG was an independent UK-based ideas studio that focused on seamless designs across a wide range of interdisciplinary media including prints, screens, and the environment. It had an international reputation for innovation, imagination, and sound commercial values.

P. 325

Bickford-Smith, Coralie

cb-smith.com

Coralie Bickford-Smith graduated in typography and graphic communication from Reading University and is currently working in-house at Penguin Books. On top of being recognised by the AIGA and D&AD, her book covers have also been featured in numerous international magazines and newspapers.

PP. 134-141

Blank

blank.com.pt

Founded by art director and graphic designer Alexandra Mendes, Blank provides creative services and design thinking by 'filling in the blanks' with fresh and provocative ideas. From concept through to completion, it focuses on content by implementing meaningful communication strategies from its base in Porto.

PP. 126-129

Boufathal, Max

Born in 1983 in Paris, Max Boufathal studied at the school of Fine Arts of Nantes where he developed a personal and unique way of conceiving his sculptures. Since then, he has created for the CAPC and the Museum of Contemporary Art of Bordeaux, amongst others. He has also participated in collective projects all over the world.

PP. 554-557

Bunch

www.bunchdesign.com

A leading London-based design studio specialising in branding, editorial design as well as digital media and motion graphics, Bunch's diverse portfolio includes work with renowned brands like BBC, Nike, Diesel, Sony, Sky, and Red Bull.

PP. 222-223

c plus c workshop

facebook.com/cpluscworkshop

c plus c workshop is a Hong Kong-based studio that focuses on graphic design, advertising, branding, corporate communications, and visual identities. In line with the philosophies behind its name — creativity and communication — the team seeks to cultivate sensitivity rather than just produce visually impressive work.

PP. 060, 206-209, 328-341

Chan, Furze

furzechan.com

Illustrator, graphic designer, and doll-maker Furze Chan lives and works in Hong Kong. Her drawings are typically characterised by a minimal composition and format. She consistently seeks the meaning of sensibility and emotions — often featuring food, animals, and found objects in her work.

PP. 096-099

Chapman-Smith, Jon / Fuman

fuman.co.nz

Jon Chapman-Smith founded Fuman in 2004 to push the boundaries of brand communication across all media. The award-winning Auckland-based creative agency offers a comprehensive array of design styles, creative direction, branding, and production services. Happiness, fresh starts, and abundance are its core visions for the clients it serves.

PP. 324, 371-373

Clarke, Chris

www.cclarke.cc

Chris Clarke is an award-winning multidisciplinary design director based in London. Currently the global deputy creative director of The Guardian, he has been recognised by the Society of News Designers, Society of Publication Designers, and D&AD, amongst others.

PP. 348-349

Collider

www.collider.com.au

A film and design collective based in Sydney, Collider functions as a hybrid between a design studio and a production/post-production/VFX company. Its multifaceted role puts it in a unique position to facilitate and foster honesty and originality for global brands, arts, and cultural organisations, as well as everything else in between.

PP. 244-247

Crescenzi, Darrin

www.dcrsnz.com

Darrin Crescenzi is an independent designer and creative director based in New York City. He creates brands, products, and experiences for various organisations – blending history with trends, technology with craft, and empathy with idealism to create design systems that are effective and inspiring.

PP. 116-117, 398-405

David, Leslie

www.leslie-david.com

Since 2010, art director Leslie David has been leading her own full-service creative studio in Paris. It provides visual and conceptual solutions for branding, print and digital designs as well as illustrations. Through collaboartion, it aims to propose creative visions and singular aesthetics to clients from the beauty, fashion, lifestyle, and music industries.

PP. 422-427

Designers United

Designers United was an award-winning multidisciplinary design firm based in Thessaloniki. Through brand identity development, creative direction, print design, as well as web design and development, it created integrated design solutions for a diverse range of international clients.

PP. 154-155

Deutsche & Japaner

deutscheundjapaner.com

Founded in 2008, Deutsche & Japaner offers expertise in graphic design, product design, interior design, illustration, and scenography as well as conceptual creation and strategic brand development. With a distinct focus on holistic solutions, its studio in Manheim places a high value on sustainable experiences.

PP. 076-079, 296-301, 304-307

Dimalla, Catherine Renee

Catherine Renee Dimalla is a multidisciplinary designer living and working in the US with a multicultural background from North America, Australia, New Zealand, and the Philippines. Her style is characterised by beautiful typography and illustrative lines.

PP. 434-441, 544

DMWORKROOM
www.dmworkroom.com

DM Workroom is a graphic design and creative studio set up by Denis Mallet, a French graphic designer and art director based in London. It solves problems using a personal, insightful, and coherent approach – matching its customers' needs with its own fundamental design and typographic principles that are characterised by flexibility and integrity.

PP. 312-315

End of Work
www.endofwork.com.au

End of Work is an Sydney-based design consultancy that prides itself on creating value for clients through creative solutions anchored by a strategic approach. Based on ideas that are 'human' and rousing, it sets out to build loyal communities, reshape mindsets, and drive business to get results.

PP. 122-125

Fons Hickmann m23

fonshickmann.com

Founded in 2001 and run by Bjoern Wolf and Fons Hickmann, Fons Hickmann m23 is an award-winning Berlin-based studio that focuses on the design of complex
communication systems mainly in the cultural field. It lends
its expertise to everything related to events, communication,
and visual identity.

PP. 414-421

Foundry

foundrystudio.com

Working with a network of talented individuals across a
range of disciplines including photography, illustration, interior design, and copywriting, Foundry is a creative agency
that takes on a collaborative approach to offer fresh, original, and tailored solutions.

PP. 072-075, 292-295

Friedman, Idan

Idan Friedman is an Israel-based product designer who
founded Reddish Studio with his partner, Naama Steinbock,
in 2002. Its aesthetic was modern and playful, with work
ranging from lighting and furniture to jewellery and home
accessories.

PP. 560-563

Futura

byfutura.com

Since it was set up in 2008 by Vicky González and Iván García, Futura in Mexico City has become an internationally renowned studio, characterised by its disruptive approach to design. Its team constantly pushes boundaries to specialise in branding, art direction, and photography – blurring the lines between different disciplines to discover new forms of creativity.

PP. 350-365

G Design Studio

gdesignstudio.gr

Located in the old city centre of Athens, G Design Studio works to facilitate public dialogue with care through multi-disciplinary projects that include strategic brand design and digital experiences. The award-winning brand design consultancy's character is reflected by the simple and clear-cut forms that usually appear in its work.

PP. 064-067

Golden

www.wearegolden.co.uk

A concept, branding, and design agency based in Leeds, Golden is led by creative director Rob Brearley, and works with clients including Nike, NBC Universal, Warner Bros., Route Publishing, and somethinksounds.

PP. 198, 524-543

GOLDENHEN

GOLDENHEN was a Melbourne-based independent creative playground established by James Goldsmith and Luke Henley. Working seamlessly across disciplines with a collaborative approach, the team strove to provide innovative and memorable experiences for clients.

PP. 370, 465-467

Greige.
greige.de

Greige. is the creative practice of Mark Kiessling and Birthe Haas in Berlin that runs on a hands-on approach and an open mind. Originally founded as an interdisciplinary design studio in 2001, its scope of work was eventually streamlined to elaborate print projects and book design.

PP. 160-165

groovisions
groovisions.com

Originally formed in Kyoto in 1993, goovisions is a design studio based in Tokyo that primarily focuses on graphics and video work. Its portfolio spans a variety of fields including music, product design, interiors, fashion, and the web.

PP. 280-283

Guang Yu

guang-yu.net

Art director, graphic designer, and AGI member Guang
Yu is the co-founder of ABlackCoverDesign in Beijing. He
has served as a jury member of the Tokyo Type Directors
Club, and has had his work recognised by D&AD and ADC,
amongst others.

PP. 130-133

Hint Creative

hintcreative.com

A creative agency and design studio focused on thoughtful
solutions for visionary brands, Hint Creative consists of a
multidisciplinary team of visual designers, art directors,
and brand strategists. Believing that little things make a big
impact, it thrives on values that are collaborative, flexible,
responsive, passionate, and grounded in purpose.

PP. 394-397

Hofstede Design

Hofstede Design was a Melbourne-based practice established in 1996. Founded by Dominic Hofstede, it specialised
in identity, publication, and environmental graphic design.
Renowned for its commitment to typographic craft, the team
strove to create effective and engaging solutions.

PP. 030-033

Homework / Jack Dahl

www.homework.dk

A creative agency and design consultancy set up in 2005, Copenhagen-based Homework specialises in brand expressions within the luxury and lifestyle industries. Once an art director for international men's fashion magazines, founder Jack Dahl has also worked with a selection of the world's most prestigious style, beauty, and luxury brands.

PP. 241–243

Jahara Studio

www.brunnojahara.com

Mixing organic shapes with tropical inspiration, Jahara Studio works across a diverse range of disciplines. Its Rio de Janeiro-based founder Brunno Jahara hopes to help his vast and multicultural country build its own design identity as a place of abundant resources, innovation, and craftsmanship.

PP. 558–559

Kao, Wei-Che

behance.net/kaoweiche

Wei-Che Kao is a graphic designer based in Taiwan who merges editorial design, graphic design, and illustration to create memorable outcomes. His portfolio consists of elegant and eye-catching book covers that are sophisticated yet striking.

PP. 474–477

KentLyons

KentLyons was a London-based design agency with a portfolio that spanned branding, digital, print, advertising, strategy, and environmental design work. Formed in 2003 by James Kent and Noel Lyons, the team sought to provide highly effective solutions that could move people.

PP. 061-063

KONG STUDIO
kong-studio.com

Kong Studio in Singapore was founded by Kevin He, a multi-disciplinary designer who specialises in art direction, visual identities, illustration, and environmental graphics. It sets out to exceed client expectations through its strength in conceptualisation and efficiency in execution.

PP. 450-455

KOTENHITS
www.hitsfamily.com

Takashi Kawada specialises in art direction for graphic, web, visual, and product creations. In 2007, he founded the creative group HITSFAMILY comprising HITSPAPER, a web magazine that explores creative relationships in society, as well as KOTENHITS, a studio that embarks on design explorations.

PP. 302-303

Kral, Tomas
tomaskral.ch

Slovakian designer Tomas Kral established his product design studio in 2008. His design approach is characterised by a clear pre-occupation for materials and processes. Taking inspiration in traditions and ordinary situations, he translates things with a touch of poetry and humour into innovative solutions and clever everyday objects.

PP. 107-111

La Tigre
latigre.net

La Tigre is an independent studio based in Milan that believes in timeless ideas. Founded in 2009, its approach is rooted in its strategic process and research, where the team converts ideas, visions, and inspirations into a system of visual expressions that elevate brands and create distinction.

PP. 516-519

lg2
lg2.com

Formerly known as lg2boutique, lg2 is currently the largest independent creative agency in Canada, with offices in Toronto, Quebec, and Montreal. In producing its award-winning, visually compelling, and strategically relevant work, it bases its creative philosophy on always seizing opportunities and creating more of them.

PP. 248-253

Lloyd and Associates

www.lloyd-associates.de

Lloyd and Associates specialises in experiential marketing, visual communications, luxury branding, and premier publishing solutions. Founded by Kimberly Lloyd, it merges disciplines driven by alternative perspectives and dynamic grids of interpretation that catalyse time-honoured design practices.

PP. 602-605

Lo Siento

www.losiento.net

Lo Siento is a Barcelona-based studio that takes an organic and physical approach to design solutions – resulting in a sweet spot where graphic and industrial design meet and dialogue. The team also enjoys finding ways to work with artisanal processes.

PP. 308-311

Luminous Design Group

www.luminous.gr

Luminous Design Group is an Athens-based storytelling studio that specialises in branding, creative direction, as well as print and digital design. The team approaches every project with passion – producing expressive, bold, and innovative work that empowers brands and realises their visions.

PP. 190-197, 199-205

MANMANTEAM Design Office Inc.

MANMANTEAM Design Office Inc. was founded by Liu Tianyang, a Qingdao-born graphic designer who is currently living and working in Beijing. It focused on print design and typography for a variety of outputs, including branding design, poster design, and publications.

PP. 224-235

Mash Creative
www.mashcreative.co.uk

Mash Creative is an independent design studio in London that was set up by Mark Bloom, a graphic- and type designer. He specialises in creative projects that include identity and branding, print media, and web design, as he searches for alternative approaches to produce unique, relevant, and successful solutions that add value to his clients' brands.

PP. 462-463

McGinness, Ryan
www.ryanmcginness.com

Born in Virginia Beach, Ryan McGinness is an artist currently based in New York. He is known for his original extensive vocabulary of graphic drawings which use the visual language of public signage, corporate logos, and contemporary iconography to create paintings, sculptures, and environments.

PP. 478-479

MEETON (Xiamen) Culture Communication Co., Ltd.

Meeton pursues and believes in original and innovative ideas to customise solutions for its clients. From its base in Xiamen, it initiates design elements that are natural during the exploration of artistic philosophies.

PP. 580-587

Michelitsch, Verena

verenamichelitsch.com

An independent graphic designer and illustrator originally from Graz, Verena Michelitsch currently specialises in branding from her base in New York City. She specialises in conceptualising and creating visual expressions spanning graphic design, art- and creative direction, illustration, as well as editorial- and digital design.

PP. 026-029

Mind Design

www.minddesign.co.uk

Founded in 1999, Mind Design is a design consultancy in London that specialises in the development of visual identities through print, web, packaging, and interior graphics. Run by Holger Jacobs and Virgile Janssen, its creative approach is based on hands-on craftsmanship, conceptual thinking, and intuition.

PP. 038-043, 520-523

mintdesigns

www.mint-designs.com

From its bases in Tokyo and Aoyama, mintdesigns aims to enrich daily life by proposing new possibilities for fashion and redefining what it means. The inspiration for its name came from the word 'mint' itself, which refers to 'brand new' or 'rare value' in English, as well as the fresh image of an herbal mint.

PP. 186-189

Mother New York

mothernewyork.com

Mother was founded in 1996 by a group of creative, free-thinking individuals 'sitting around a kitchen table eating lunch'. With offices across London, New York, Los Angeles, Shanghai, and 'the oddly Shoreditch-based continent of South America', it works across advertising, brand design, interactive experiences, and content development.

PP. 442-445

Mucho

wearemucho.com

From its offices in Barcelona, Paris, San Francisco, New York, and Sydney, Mucho's work spans various disciplines to include art direction, strategic identity design, editorial design, packaging design, graphic communications, digital design, and motion graphics.

PP. 034-037, 178-185, 506-507

Murmure

murmure.me

Based in Caen and Paris, Murmure is a French creative communications agency specialising in strong visual identities. Led by Julien Alirol Ressencourt and Paul, it focuses on singular creative projects with aesthetics adapted to its clients' aims and objectives. The agency strives to make original work that it can be proud of.

PP. 510-511

MyOrb

myorbstudio.com

Specialists in making things that are curious, intriguing, and playful, MyOrb is a design studio based in New York. The team focuses on creating mutually-beneficial relationships with clients in a variety of industries such as art, culture, architecture, media, and fashion.

PP. 488-491

Nelson Associates

nelsonassociates.co.uk

A Surrey-based design studio founded by Christian Nelson, Nelson Associates has a reputation for creating thoughtful, considered, and beautiful designs. The team works closely with a network of award-winning collaborators to create relevant, powerful, and commercially effective work for each and every client.

PP. 284-291

Nendesign inc.

www.nendesign.net

Originally just a creative team in London in 2007, Yoshihiro Yoshida and Shiho Kikuchi established the Nendesign inc. studio in 2009 after returning to Japan. The team does not believe that all of its designs have to be liked by everyone, but instead, be pure and full of soul.

PP. 508-509

Neubau

neubauberlin.com

Defined by a systematic approach to type as well as print, screen, and space design, Berlin-based Neubau was founded by Stefan Gandl in 2001. Besides releasing bestselling books like 'Neubau Welt' (2005), 'Neubau Modul' (2007), and 'Neubau Forst Catalogue' (2014), Stefan has also had his works internationally exhibited and published.

PP. 564-567

Nilsson, Jens

www.jens-nilsson.com

Jens Nilsson is a Stockholm-based, award-winning graphic designer, art director, and 'great guy' with over 10 years of industry experience. He strives to create expressive and ambitious visual concepts within the fields of branding, packaging, typography, still life photography, print design and digital environments for both small and big businesses.

PP. 568-575

Nippon Design Center, Inc.

www.ndc.co.jp

Founded in 1959, Nippon Design Center, Inc. continually seeks new challenges to provide clients with the highest quality design, where 'the work is identifying the fundamental nature of a thing, and the skill is fashioning a visible form for it'. Its network spans across Tokyo, Nagoya, and Beijing.

PP. 100-105

Penique Productions

peniqueproductions.com

Penique Productions was born in 2007. It is a collective of artists of different disciplines focused on a common project which is based on the idea of making ephemeral installations. Founded by Sergi Arbusà, Pablo Baqué, Chamo San, and Pol Clusella, it now operates from offices in Barcelona and Rio de Janeiro.

PP. 606-611

Peregrín, Paco

www.pacoperegrin.com

Based in Madrid but working globally, Paco Peregrín is a visual artist and award-winning photographer who specialises in fashion, beauty, art, and advertising for brands. His work has been featured in renowned publications such as Vogue and Harper's Bazaar, as well as exhibitions all around the world.

PP. 366-369

Peter Tarka Design
www.petertarka.com

An award-winning artist, art director, and illustrator currently
based in London, Peter Tarka is able to craft mesmerising
and surrealistic visual experiences. He produces immer-
sive illustrations using forms, shapes, and bold colours to
elevate aesthetics for the most recognisable brands on the
planet, including Apple, Nike, Adobe, and Heineken.

PP. 268-271

Plenty
www.plenty.tv

Founded by Mariano Farias and Pablo Alfieri in 2010, Plenty is
an art and motion direction company based in Buenos Aires.
Its team consists of designers, illustrators, as well as 2D
and 3D animators working with different techniques to bring
hyper-realistic stop-motion and animation projects to life. Its
client list includes FOX, MTV, Schweppes, Vodafone, and Bic.

P. 272-279, 456-457

Pop & Pac Studio
www.pop-pac.com

Melbourne-based Pop & Pac has a passion for all things
design. Together with its clients and collaborators, the studio
makes brands stand out through design and holistically
experiential creative executions. The team's capabilities encompass identity creation, strategy, print media, and more.

PP. 380-393

Present & Correct

www.presentandcorrect.com

Opening its virtual doors in 2008, Present & Correct aims to share its long-term obsession with stationery, paper, and office objects inspired by homework, post offices, and schools. It offers an online shopping wonderland for the brand's original designs as well as other international designers' products, alongside vintage items collected from all over Europe.

PP. 010-011

Proctor, Yogi

yogiproctor.com

Yogi Proctor holds a BA in Visual and Critical Studies from The School The Art Institute of Chicago, and an MA in Aesthetics and Politics from CalArts. His work has been shown at The Poor Farm in Wisconsin, La Gaite in Paris, Green Gallery at Yale School of Art in Connecticut, Times Square Gallery at Hunter College in New York, and Seeline Gallery in Los Angeles.

PP. 504-505

Rice Creative

rice-creative.com

Rice Creative is a Ho Chi Minh City-based creative agency that was founded in 2011 by Joshua Breiden Bach and Chi-An De Leo. A multicultural team creating honest and powerful creative solutions, it sets out to bring high value to bold brands through singular ideas, backed by conviction and acclaimed craft.

PP. 044-051

Ritator

Stockholm-based Ritator was a design and advertising agency that was founded in 2007 by Gustav Granström, Oscar Laufersweiler, and Andreas Högberg. Through graphic design, it deployed unique concepts to create attention and interest for clients in the commercial and public sector.

PP. 496-499

Sarin, Tong

Inspired by everyday happenings and images of the old days, Tong Sarin creates peculiar scenes out of ordinary events by fusing raw Thai humour with western commercial styles. He is always in search of comedic and groundbreaking ideas to execute, and his ultimate reward is laughter from his audience.

PP. 458-461

SEA
www.seadesign.com

An award-winning brand communications agency in London working across a variety of disciplines including brand strategy and positioning, corporate identity design, art direction, and digital media development, SEA helps a wide range of clients grow and develop by harnessing good design.

PP. 080-087

Sitoh inc.
www.sitoh.co.jp

Sitoh inc. seeks to bring individuals, cultures, and societies together through the power of design. Established in 2016 by Motoi Shito, the studio produces dynamic and effective graphics that communicate its ideas. Its diverse design portfolio encompasses products, packaging, books, websites, fashion, advertising, and video artwork.

PP. 598-601

Slanted Magazine & Weblog
www.slanted.de

Slanted Publishers is an international publishing and media house founded by Lars Harmsen and Julia Kahl in Germany. Its award-winning print magazine Slanted covers international developments in design and culture twice a year as well as other design-related projects in the field of typography, contemporary art, and design.

PP. 446-449

Sova Magazine
sova-magazine.com

An independent art magazine that was founded in 2009 in Malmö, Sova features unknown and upcoming creatives with an array of divisive, hedonistic, and intimate points of view. Underlining contemporary discourse, every issue showcases divergent narratives, empathies, and their refractions.

P. 545

Strategy Design & Advertising

www.strategythinking.com

Strategy Design & Advertising is an independent and award-winning full-service design-led advertising agency with a team of talented and passionate people across offices in New Zealand, Australia, and Japan. It produces consistent and effective communications through smart thinking, impeccable craft, and client relationships.

PP. 512-515

Studio Band

studioband.com.au

A graphic design consultancy based in Adelaide, Studio Band specialises in the creation and development of dynamic and unique graphic solutions that engage and connect with audiences. The team works closely with clients to build trusting relationships – delivering thoughtful, intelligent, and strategic solutions under a high level of execution and integrity.

PP. 322-323

Studio Job

www.studio-job.com

Studio Job was founded in 1998 by Job Smeets, combining traditional and modern techniques to produce once-in-a-lifetime objects. It has crafted a body of work that draws upon classical, popular, and contemporary design as well as highly visual and sculptural art.

PP. 546-553

STUDIO NEWWORK

studionewwork.com

A branding and creative studio based in New York, STU-DIO NEWWORK assembles passionate type designers with a commitment to excellence in design. Besides working across a range of media spanning print, screen graphics, products, and environmental design, it has also published NEWWORK MAGAZINE, a large-format arts publication.

PP. 596-597

Sugar Paper Los Angeles

sugarpaper.com

Established in 2003 by graphic designers Chelsea Shukov and Jamie Grobecker, Sugar Paper creates delicate statio-nery with a strong sense of nostalgia – shining a spotlight on a beautiful and underappreciated art form. Each product is seen as a distinct statement about one's individual style.

PP. 020-025

Takt Studio

taktstudio.com

Takt Studio specialises in developing strategy-driven cre-ative ideas for new and existing brands. From commercial work to non-profit projects, the Melbourne-based agency combines strategic thinking with insightful design to deliver effective communication across multiple platforms.

PP. 118-121, 254

Tamborrino, Giada

gtstudio.co

Giada Tamborrino is a freelance graphic designer in Amsterdam who is passionate about creativity in all its forms and expressions. Through her eponymous studio, she enjoys helping sustainable brands come to life and collaborating with forward-thinking people through intentional and meaningful design.

PP. 052-059

Tsagaris, Panos

panostsagaris.com

'Panos Tsagaris' photographic work aims to transcend traditional practices of imagery by incorporating existing materials with transformative processes –producing symbolic objects that underline humanity's individual and collective struggle with spiritual development.' (Maria Nicolacopoulou) Born in Athens, he currently lives and works in New York.

PP. 406-413

ujidesign

ujidesign.com

Founded in 2005 by award-winning art director Yutaka Maeda, ujidesign is a creative studio based in Tokyo. Its range of services span across graphic design, packaging, way-finding, and book design to web design and development.

PP. 142-153

UnderConsideration LLC

underconsideration.com

Run by Bryony Gomez-Palacio and Armin Vit in Bloomington, UnderConsideration LLC is a graphic design firm that generates its own projects, initiatives, and content while taking on limited client work. Its Brand New blog was launched in 2006 and has grown to be the leading site for opinions on design.

PP. 166-177

Westermann, Sara

www.sarawestermann.com

Sara Westermann is a Portuguese multidisciplinary graphic designer who specialises in posters, editorial design, illustration, photography, and art direction. Currently based in Germany, she has worked mainly in artistic and cultural mediums for notable companies like Inditex, one of the world's largest fashion retailers.

PP. 428-433

Wilhelmson Arkitekter

Founded by Swedish architect Anders Wilhelmson in 1989, Wilhelmson Arkitekter (formerly Wilhelmson Architects AB) was an architectural practice best known for its internationally acclaimed works such as the funerary chapel for the Ciula family in Viterbo, the EOS residential housing project in Helsingborg, and the new city of Kiruna.

PP. 612-615

WILLOW

WILLOW was the creative guise of designer Will Connor. Its fundamental approach was based on an appreciation for the formidable marriage of image and text, a propensity for eclectic aesthetics, an obsession with detail, as well as a love of the diverse.

PP. 594-595

Winkreative
www.winkreative.com

The Winkreative team prides itself on creating value enhancement for its clients through creative solutions anchored by a quality journalistic approach, as well as an intuitive entrepreneurial extension of design and craft credentials. From its offices across the world, it makes brands desirable through elegant visual ideas and a distinctive tone of voice.

PP. 576-577

WORK
workwerk.com

WORK is a multidisciplinary design agency founded by Theseus Chan in Singapore. His team strives to create work that is provocative yet relevant for renowned brands in bringing 'more art into design', with past clients including the likes of Louis Vuitton–Yayoi Kusama, adidas Originals, and Comme des Garçons.

PP. 480-487

Work in Progress

workinprogress.no

Specialising in graphic design, branding, art direction, and packaging, Work in Progress is a Norwegian multidisciplinary design studio that creates effective and captivating design solutions based on conceptual thinking with great attention to detail and high levels of craft and finishing.

PP. 578-579

Acknowledgements

We would like to specially thank all the designers and studios who are featured in this book for their significant contribution towards its compilation. We would also like to express our deepest gratitude to our producers for their invaluable advice and assistance throughout this project, as well as the many professionals in the creative industry who were generous with their insights, feedback, and time. To those whose input was not specifically credited or mentioned here, we truly appreciate your support.

Future Editions

If you wish to participate in viction:ary's future projects and publications, please send your portfolio to:
submit@victionary.com